D1584362

PARIS

REDISCOVERED

CAROLINE DELABROY

Paris Rediscovered
Published by Lonely Planet Publications Pty Ltd
ABN 36 005 607 983

Australia (Head Office)	Locked Bag 1, Footscray, Vic 3011 ☎ 03 8379 8000 fax 03 8379 8111
USA	150 Linden St, Oakland, CA 94607 ☎ 510 250 6400 toll free 800 275 8555 fax 510 893 8572
UK	2nd fl, 186 City Rd London EC1V 2NT ☎ 020 7106 2100 fax 020 7106 2101
Contact	talk2us@lonelyplanet.com lonelyplanet.com/contact

This title was produced by:
Place des Éditeurs: Director Frédérique Sarfati-Romano **Editor** Didier Férat **Editorial Coordinator (French)** Juliette Stephens **Editorial Coordinator (English)** Émeline Gontier **Translated from French to English** Emma Duffy, Emma Hearle, Michael Scott **Graphical Coordinator** Jean-Noël Doan **Sketches** Laurence Tixier **Maps** Nicolas Chauveau **Photography** Jean-François Tripelon **Cover** Sarbacane Design **Lonely Planet: Regional Publisher** Imogen Hall **Coordinating Editor** Alison Ridgway **Mapping** Mark Griffiths **Layout Designer** Mazzy Prinsep **Managing Editor** Liz Heynes **Managing Layout Designers** Indra Kilfoyle, Celia Wood **Thanks to** Brendan Dempsey, Alison Lyall, Darren O'Connell.

All images are copyright of the photographers unless otherwise indicated. Many of the images in this guide are available for licensing from Lonely Planet Images: lonelyplanetimages.com

ISBN 978-1-74220-555-7

Printed by Hang Tai Printing Company, Hong Kong
Printed in China

Acknowledgements Many thanks to the following for the use of their content: Paris Metro Map © 2010 RATP

MIX
Paper from
responsible sources
FSC™ C021741
www.fsc.org

Editor's acknowledgements
The editor would like to thank the Paris Île-de-France Tourist Board for its support. For more information about what's in and what's on in Paris and Île-de-France, go to www.new-paris-idf.com

HOW TO USE THIS BOOK
Colour codes and maps

The colour symbols represent places and businesses mentioned in the book and are marked on the appropriate maps for ease of reference. For example, restaurants are shown as a green fork. Each neighbourhood is given a colour which is used for the tabs in the chapter devoted to it.

Prices

The € symbols in this guide show the cost of a meal – main course, starter or dessert – for one person excluding alcoholic drinks.

€	< €16
€€	€16-30
€€€	€30-50
€€€€	> €50

Send Us Your Feedback We love to hear from travellers – your comments keep us on our toes and help make our books better. Our well-travelled team reads every word on what you loved or loathed about this book. Although we cannot reply individually to postal submissions, we always guarantee that your feedback goes straight to the appropriate authors, in time for the next edition. Each person who sends us information is thanked in the next edition, and the most useful submissions are rewarded with a free book.

Visit **lonelyplanet.com** to submit your updates and suggestions or to ask for help. Our award-winning website also features inspirational travel stories, news and discussions.

Note: We may edit, reproduce and incorporate your comments in Lonely Planet products such as guidebooks, websites and digital products, so let us know if you don't want your comments reproduced or your name acknowledged. For a copy of our privacy policy visit **lonelyplanet.com/privacy**.

THIS IS PARIS

How well do you know the Paris Île-de-France region? On your first visit, you are sure to have seen monuments, famous avenues and a wealth of timeless, unforgettable sights…which we're not going to repeat here! The aim of this guide is for you to rediscover the area. We will give you a more intimate picture of a city in motion where there is always something new to see.

From the cosmopolitan Canal Saint-Martin to the groundbreaking architecture of the 13th and the major new museums in the west of the capital to the burgeoning, creative northeast…Paris Île-de-France always has something different and sometimes completely unexpected to offer.

The Parc de la Villette and its surrounding areas provide visitors with a huge space for cultural activities or just relaxing with the family. The MAC/VAL puts on the best creative talent on the outskirts of the city and fashion designers of the moment display their wares in the Upper Marais, not far from the Rue Montorgueil with its shops and cafés.

Restaurants revamped by the big names in French design provide you with intimate places to meet or if you're in the mood to party, head to the bars and clubs in Belleville or Montreuil, which are a hit among Parisians.

All these great places have been listed in this guide. You will also find new ways of exploring this melting pot of cultures and trends and meet the men and women who live in the city and help to shape it. It's now up to you to go out and see this 'new Paris Île-de-France' for yourself!

Photographs All photographs: CRT Paris Île-de-France/Tripelon-Jarry, except p6, p8 (right), p10 (left) Lonely Planet Images/ Olivier Cirendini; p8 left Lonely Planet Images/John Banagan; p9 left Lonely Planet Images/Jean-Bernard Carillet, right Lonely Planet Images/Izzet Keribar; p10 right Lonely Planet Images/Dan Herrick; p11 left Lonely Planet Images/Will Salter, right Lonely Planet Images/Jean-Bernard Carillet; p12 Lonely Planet Images/Elliot Daniel; p26 Lonely Planet Images/Anne Dowie; p29 Lonely Planet Images/Will Salter; p36 Lonely Planet Images/Russell Mountford; p53 Lonely Planet Images/John Elk III; p63 Miller; p85 Lonely Planet Images/Jean-Bernard Carillet; p90 Martin Argyroglo; p92 Lonely Planet Images/Oliver Strewe; p98 & p103 Lonely Planet Images/Will Salter; p123 Véronique Tarka Partouche; p150 Thierry Nava. **Cover photograph** Lonely Planet Images/Will Salter. All photographs are covered by the photographers' copyrights unless indicated otherwise.

THE AUTHOR

CAROLINE DELABROY

Caroline was born in the 13th arrondissement on the Paris Left Bank and grew up in a well-heeled suburb before returning to Paris as a student. Since her university days, she has crossed the Seine to live on the Right Bank behind the Butte Montmartre and has never gone back. She may do so one day, but for now Caroline has settled on this side of Paris which admittedly is not perfect, but boasts a whole host of regular haunts, quirky spots and hidden gems. Through her work for Lonely Planet, Caroline has combed the streets of Paris both on foot and by Vélib' hire bike in between trips to the Basque Country, Bordeaux and Québec. She has also written about trendy spots in Paris for other publications and interviewed entrepreneurs in the Île-de-France, whilst reporting on current affairs for the France 24 website. Caroline is still passionate about the capital.

ACKNOWLEDGEMENTS

Thanks to all at Lonely Planet and in particular Didier Férat for his insatiable curiosity, trust and time, and to Juliette Stephens for her keen eye and the thorough job she has done of editing the guide. Thanks also to Bénédicte Houdré whose fantastic work on the Petit Voyage guide, *La Villette et le Nord-Est Parisien* served as an inspiration for many sections of this book. My thanks also go to the Paris Île-de-France Tourist Board for its superb initiative, useful information and responsive staff. Finally, I'd like to thank everyone who spared some time to provide me with information and share their passion.

CONTRIBUTOR
BÉNÉDICTE HOUDRÉ

When she's not writing a Lonely Planet guide, Bénédicte spends her time exploring Paris. From museums to alternative exhibitions, bars, concert halls, art galleries and theatres, she delves into the fashions of Paris, looking for that gem – a trendy boutique tucked away at the end of a side street, an art gallery in an unusual location or a bar with authentic charm. Not forgetting the pleasure she also gets from meeting people during her explorations.

CONTENTS

Go to Paris at any time of the year and there will always be something going on in the city or suburbs. Countless festivals take place throughout the year, peaking in spring and summer when concerts spring up in the street, parks and other unlikely locations. The Fête de la Musique (summer music festival) and other events such as the Nuit Blanche (all-night artfest), the Nuit des Musées (museum night) and Paris Plages (for beachlovers), catering to all, whether art lovers or party animals, have in recent years become hits among Parisians. We have only provided a selection of events here: there is plenty more to investigate. For up-to-date listings, check out the website www.new-paris-idf.com. A full schedule of events also appears every Wednesday in *Pariscope* and *L'Officiel des Spectacles* sold in newsagents and news-stands.

Marche des Fiertes (Gay Pride; p10)

PARIS DIARY

Chinese New Year celebrations

Grande Arche, location for festival chorus

JANUARY

Chinese New Year

www.paris.fr

Between the end of January and the beginning of February, dragons swirl through the streets and Chinese lanterns are lit between the Place d'Italie and the Porte de Choisy in the 13th arrondissement, the main Chinese neighbourhood in Paris.

Sales

On from January to February (and July to August), a rare chance to treat yourself to the creativity and savoir-faire of Parisian designers and brands at knockdown prices.

FEBRUARY

Carnaval de Paris

http://carnavaldeparis.org

At the beginning of February, a lively and colourful procession warms up the streets of Paris with medieval carnival spirit.

MARCH

Banlieues Bleues

www.banlieuesbleues.org

In March and April, five weeks of jazz, blues, world, soul, funk and R'n'B concerts are organised in Saint-Denis and the surrounding area, where famous artists perform on stage or in the street.

Festival Chorus

www.chorus92.fr

At the end of March, *chanson* (French song) is performed live by famous artists and young talents. The festival village is set up at the foot of the Grande Arche in La Défense.

APRIL

Villette Sonique

www.villettesonique.com

Running from late May to early June, La Villette hosts a week of concerts and events celebrating rock, electro and other music

La Geode, Parc de la Villette

Art installation in Orsay Museum

genres both in the Grande Halle and its surrounding gardens.

MAY

Les Puces du Design
www.pucesdudesign.com
In May and October, antique dealers use the Bassin de la Villette as a backdrop to their wares including furniture, accessories and clothes from the 1950s to the 1980s.

La Nuit des Musées
www.nuitdesmusees.culture.fr
From 7pm to 1am one Saturday in May, special lighting, musical performances, plays and readings are arranged to complement the permanent collections in Paris museums.

La Force de l'Art
www.forcedelart.culture.fr
Running from May to June, this festival, taking place every three years, presents a broad spectrum of French contemporary art. Over 200 artists exhibit work in the Nave of the Grand Palais. Organised alternate years with the *Monumenta* exhibition (www .monumenta.com, see p46).

Open Studios
www.ateliers-artistes-belleville.org
http://les-frigos.com
www.ateliersdemenilmontant.org
www.anversauxabbesses.fr
www.montmartre-aux-artistes.org
Belleville artists are the first to open their work space to the public, kicking off a season of open access to studios in the Frigos (May), Père Lachaise (May), Ménilmontant (September) and Montmartre (October to December).

Rencontres Chorégraphiques Internationales de Seine-Saint-Denis
www.rencontreschoregraphiques.com
Performances from established or up-and-coming contemporary dance troupes. The

Marche des Fiertés (Gay Pride) parade

Soldiers, Bastille Day parade

Centre National de la Danse (p136) in Pantin is one of the venues hosting the festival.

JUNE

Designer's Days
www.designersdays.com
Discover the world of fashion over four days in temporary exhibitions at selected boutiques and showrooms around the city.

Marche des Fiertés (Gay Pride)
http://marche.inter-lgbt.org
A lively procession proclaiming lesbian, gay, bisexual and transvestite pride, between Denfert-Rochereau and Bastille.

Fête de la Musique
http://fetedelamusique.culture.fr
On 21 June, to mark the summer solstice, there are concerts in every town, taking place in streets, gardens, bars and cafés.

Festival de Saint-Denis
www.festival-saint-denis.com
A classical and world-music festival with more than 20 concerts in the Basilique de Saint-Denis and other venues around the town.

Solidays
www.solidays.org
Three days of concerts are held at the Paris-Longchamp racecourse to raise money for AIDS charities, with artists from across the musical spectrum.

Paris Jazz Festival
www.parisjazzfestival.net
Free live jazz at the Parc Floral every Saturday and Sunday afternoon in June and July.

JULY

Bastille Day (14 July)
Military parade from 8.30am on the Champs-Élysées and fireworks over the Champs-de-Mars at around 11pm. There are also dances held at fire-stations the night before.

Paris Cinéma
www.pariscinema.org
This festival is a showcase for contemporary cinema in Paris and features 15 full-length films (fiction and documentary) as part of an international competition. The films are screened to invited audiences at various locations around Paris, both in cinemas and in the open-air.

Sunbathers, Paris Plages

Paris Plages
www.paris.fr / www.lefestivalfnac.com
From the end of July to the end of August, Parisians hit the beach on the Voie Georges Pompidou, the Quai de la Gare and the Bassin de la Villette. Free concerts are organised for the Indédendances festival.

Cinéma en Plein Air
www.villette.com
From mid-July to mid-August, films are shown outdoors daily in Parc de la Villette. All films are shown in original version with subtitles.

AUGUST

Paris Quartier d'Été
www.quartierdete.com
Dance, music, theatre, circus acts and other activities in parks, squares, avenues and around monuments from mid-July to August.

Rock en Seine
www.rockenseine.com
At the end of August, rock music hits the Parc de Saint-Cloud with three days of concerts

Jazz musicians, Le Caveau de la Huchette

including a whole host of international headliners.

SEPTEMBER

Festival d'Automne
www.festival-automne.com
A dance, music, theatre and plastic arts festival which takes place throughout autumn in different locations around the capital.

Jazz à la Villette
www.citedelamusique.fr
Jazz festival lasting around 10 days in the Parc de la Villette and the Cité de la Musique.

Techno Parade
www.technoparade.fr
A parade devoted to house and electro culture.

OCTOBER

Nuit Blanche

www.paris.fr

At the beginning of October, contemporary art lovers can spend the whole night visiting various venues around Paris, absolutely free of charge.

Foire Internationale d'Art Contemporain

www.fiac.com

At the end of October, you can get your fill of contemporary art in the Nave of the Grand Palais and in the Cour Carrée at the Louvre.

Le Passe Muraille by Jean Marais, rue Norvins

NOVEMBER

Mois de la Photo

www.mep-fr.org

Over 60 exhibitions on a common theme in galleries, museums and cultural centres. Takes place on even years (Photoquai, a two-yearly festival of photographs from around the world is staged on odd years). This event coincides with Paris Photo (www.parisphoto .fr), an annual photography festival at the Carrousel du Louvre.

Festival des Inrocks

http://festival.lesinrocks.com

This festival organised by the magazine *Les Inrockuptibles* features a line-up of up-and-coming artists from around the world.

It takes place in various venues around Paris (La Cigale, La Boule Noire, Olympia, la Maroquinerie et le Point Éphémère).

DECEMBER

Africolor

www.africolor.com

Between mid-November and the end of December, this festival features urban music from Africa and the Indian Ocean. Takes place in a number of towns around Seine-Saint-Denis.

Semaine du Fooding

www.lefooding.com

A week of events on the theme of Fooding® (a blend of the words 'food' and 'feeling'), all in the aim of making food fun.

Find out more about Paris Île-de-France's events on www.new-paris-idf.com.

>SNAPSHOTS

MK2 Cinema, Bassin de la Villette (p135)

MAC/VAL (p81)

>1 CONTEMPORARY ART

The Pompidou Centre (p29), the Jeu de Paume (p32) and the Maison Européenne de la Photographie (p98) were the first arrivals on the contemporary art scene in and around Paris. These were the first to exhibit contemporary work and to expose young artists and new creative techniques to the public.

Today, a vast array of the hottest contemporary art is dotted all around the city. Its museums, foundations, galleries, art centres, art colleges (most famously the École Nationale Supérieure des Beaux-Arts), squats and non-profit organisations make Paris Île-de-France the centre of the French art world. Several of these venues have become landmarks and attract a wide audience, such as the Palais de Tokyo (p44), the Cartier Foundation (p65), the MAC/VAL museum (p81) in Vitry-sur-Seine, or the CENTQUATRE (p137). Gallery owners such as Yvon Lambert (p98) and Marian Goodman (p99), whose galleries cluster in the Marais, Pompidou Centre, Rue de Seine and Rue Louise-Weiss areas, have gained an international reputation.

The latest creative trends can be found in places like Le Cube in Issy-les-Moulineaux (p71), the Laboratoires d'Aubervilliers (p137) or the Ferme du Buisson in Noisiel (p144). Paris is also home to several important events such as Fiac and Paris Photo. Go to www.new-paris-idf.com to find up-to-date information on contemporary art exhibitions and events.

Passage Brady (p59)

>2 MULTICULTURAL PARIS

Paris Île-de-France owes its diversity as a region to the fact that it boasts cultures from every continent, as illustrated by Évry, a new town, home to numerous ethnic communities, with no less than five places of worship belonging to different world religions (p147). You could almost travel the world without leaving the region. To immerse yourself in an African atmosphere, head to Château Rouge and the Dejean Market, where countless items arrive straight from that continent: okra, peppers, cassava or dried fish, not to mention certain cosmetics and rolls of brightly coloured fabrics.

Indian, Pakistani and Turkish communities live side by side in the Rue du Faubourg-Saint-Denis, where you'll find many restaurants offering their traditional food. The Passage Brady (p59) has great Indian restaurants. There are more to be found on Rue Cail, a couple of streets above the Gare du Nord. The Asian communities live in the 13th arrondissement (check out the Tang Frères supermarket), Belleville, Ivry and Alfortville with its amazing Chinagora hotel. The markets in Belleville (p108), Montreuil (p95) and Saint-Denis (p125) are cosmopolitan areas, adding to the region's multicultural feel. Africolor (p12) and the Festival de Saint-Denis (p10) are major highlights on the calendar.

If you want to find out more about the history of the immigrants who have settled in the region, head to the new Cité Nationale de l'Histoire de l'Immigration (p88).

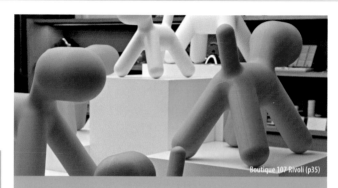
Boutique 107 Rivoli (p35)

>3 INTERIOR DESIGN

In Paris, interior design is now showcased in style with the newly renovated Musée des Arts Décoratifs (p29), and the opening of the Lieu du Design (p90), but it's not all about museums. Pieces are now filtering down to become a part of the city's everyday surroundings. Restaurants and bars (see the unique Phillipe Starck furniture at Kong, p38), hotels (Andrée Putman at Pershing Hall or Christophe Pillet at Sezz) and even cinemas (see Martin Szekely's love seat at MK2) and car showrooms (on the Champs-Élysées) are calling on designers to turn their spaces into something remarkable.

The term design art is being used more often today. Like their counterparts in the 1950s (including Prouvé, Perriand and Le Corbusier), contemporary furniture designers such as Ronan and Erwan Bouroullec, Andrea Branzi and Marc Newson have met with great success in galleries (the Kreo gallery takes particular credit for its contribution, see p68). Institutions such as the Mobilier National (p69) and the Cité de la Céramique à Sèvres (sevresciteceramique.fr; Place de la Manufacture, Sèvres; M Pont-de-Sèvres) have links with these designers. VIA, an association promoting interior design innovation, aims to unite designers and manufacturers and has a gallery underneath the Viaduc des Arts (p88). Events like the Puces du Design (p9) or Designer's Days (p10) are highly popular. You can also buy interior design items in shops at quite reasonable prices: try Sentou (p71), Lieu Commun (p101) or Galeries Lafayette Maison.

Le Showcase (p 51)

>4 NIGHTLIFE IN PARIS

So what is nightlife in Paris like compared to what's on offer in nearby London or Barcelona? Parisians like to ask themselves this question, as – contrary to popular belief – they do care about their reputation outside France. Looking at the sheer number of places available for night outings, from intimate bars offering live music to the hippest clubs, there is no doubt that Paris is alive and well. Perhaps things are a little different here, but the city is definitely happening.

Places to go depend on the crowd you belong to: from bourgeois bohemians to rock, techno and electro fans, there is something for everyone. The Rex Club (p62) is still the place to go for electro nights and has the hottest DJs, while party animals head to places like the Nouveau Casino (p114) or the Flèche d'Or (p113) for their eclectic mix of music. There is also a fashion for small, friendly clubs like Le Baron (p51), which are changing the fabric of the city's nightlife. More alternative venues exist as well, such as the Point Éphémère (p61), the Instants Chavirés (p95) in Montreuil or the Mains d'Œuvres (p129) in Saint-Ouen. However, fashionable bars still remain the most popular venues in Parisian nightlife, especially on Rue Oberkampf and Rue Ménilmontant in the 11th arrondissement. These bars are usually where the night starts and ends.

Extensive listings for night-time events in Paris can be found on www.new-paris-idf.com.

Docks en Seine (p 79)

>5 CONTEMPORARY ARCHITECTURE

Paris is falling over itself in the race to produce new architecture. Although the Pompidou Centre, the Bibliothèque Nationale de France, the Louvre pyramid, the Cartier Foundation and the Grande Arche de la Défense have earned their reputations, there are other, more recent buildings competing for the same recognition. The Docks en Seine (p79) owe their steel and painted glass façade to the architects Jakob + MacFarlane. In their own special ways, the Simone de Beauvoir footbridge (by Dietmar Feichtinger, p78), the MAC/VAL (Jacques Ripault and Denise Duhart, p81), the university campus on the site of the former Paris windmills (Rudy Ricciotti and Nicolas Michelin, p78) and the Masséna neighbourhood (Christian de Portzamparc) are all examples of sustainable, urban architecture.

The name Jean Nouvel crops up in many of these projects, such as the Musée du quai Branly, (p44), the Signal de la Défense and the building intended to house the Paris Philharmonic Orchestra (p135). However, his is not the only name worth mentioning. The huge 'canopy' project (p32) to cover the Forum des Halles has been entrusted to Patrick Berger and Jacques Anziutti. Rudy Ricciotti will be designing the new Jean-Bouin stadium and Frank Gehry will be working on the Fondation Louis Vuitton (in progress). To get a better idea of contemporary architecture in and around Paris, visit the Cité de l'Architecture et du Patrimoine (p 47) and the Pavillon de l'Arsenal (p88).

La Maroquinerie (p 114)

>6 THE PARIS MUSIC SCENE

Although large mainstream concerts take place in the Stade de France (p 120) or Bercy stadium (p77), there are countless smaller, more intimate music venues around the city. Jazz fans look out for concerts at the Baiser salé (p33), the New Morning (p62), the Duc des Lombards (☎ 01 42 33 22 88; www.ducdeslombards.com; 42 Rue des Lombards, 1st), the Sunset-Sunside (p40), and the Bizz'art (p62). La Dynamo (☎ 01 49 22 10 10; www.banlieuesbleues.org; 9 Rue G.-Josserand, Pantin) was the first venue in France set up specially for jazz and improvised music.

La Villette has a lot to offer music-wise, with both the Cité de la Musique (p134) and venues as diverse as Le Zénith (☎ 0890 71 02 07; www.le-zenith.com), Trabendo (p141), Cabaret Sauvage (p140) and Glaz'art (p141). Rue Boyer, in Ménilmontant, is another good place to go, with La Maroquinerie (p114), La Bellevilloise (p114) and Le Café des Sports (p113). Also worth a visit is the northern part of the Canal Saint-Martin, home to Le Point Éphémère (p61). Just below the Bibliothèque Nationale, there are live-music boats moored on the river: the Batofar (p82) plays electro, while the Dame de Canton (p83) tends to play more world music.

The Social Club (p61), the Café La Pêche (☎ 01 48 70 69 65; www.lapechecafe .com; 16 rue Pépin, Montreuil) and Le Tamanoir (☎ 01 47 98 03 63; www.letamanoir .com; 27 Av Lucette-Mazalaigue, Gennevilliers) are great spots to hear the latest sounds, while Pop In (p94) and the Flèche d'Or (p113) are good indie rock venues. Le Bataclan (☎ 01 43 14 00 30; www.myspace.com/bataclanparis; 50 Bd Voltaire, 11th), La Cigale (☎ 01 49 25 81 75; www.lacigale.fr; 120 Bd Rochechouart, 18th) and the Café de la Danse (☎ 01 47 00 57 59; 5 Passage Louis-Philippe, 11th) also have good gig listings. Finally, Les Trois Baudets (p128) is dedicated to the new style of French *chansons*. Each summer, find out all about Paris festivals on www.new-paris-idf.com.

Série Limitée, Montmartre (p124)

>7 PARISIAN FASHION

Style in Paris is all about fashion with a twist, which nonetheless manages to look timelessly chic. Trailblazing designers such as Stefano Pilati for YSL, Nicolas Ghesquière for Balenciaga, Gaspard Yurkievich, Christian Lacroix, Jean-Paul Gaultier, Martin Margiela, Marithé and François Girbaud and many others need no introduction. However, young ready-to-wear designers are showing that they too can be creative and moreover accessible, tapping into the style of Parisian women who pull off a seamless mix of contradictory feminine, urban and ethnic pieces. Vanessa Bruno (p70) and Isabel Marant (p90) were the first to pioneer this with flair.

Parisian fashion is more than ever about the freedom to play mix and match with prices, such as pairing a top from H&M or Uniqlo with designer jeans, or vice-versa. For fashion and shopping heaven, go to Galeries Lafayette (www.galerieslafayette.com; 1st floor; Bd Haussmann, 9th) or Printemps Haussmann (www.printemps.com; 2nd floor, 64 Bd Haussmann, 9th) which both have designer sections. Paris is also home to numerous private stylists whose showrooms you can visit to see them at work, such as Beau Travail (p109), or try the Rue Houdon (p124) in Montmartre and the Rue des Gardes (p124) in the Goutte d'Or neighbourhood.

Vélib' hire point (p 159)

>8 DIFFERENT WAYS TO GET AROUND

The best way to discover Paris and the Île-de-France is to take public transport. As well as the extensive bus, metro and RER network, there are now other great new alternatives to driving. By far and away the most popular initiative has been the city's new self-access bicycle hire system, Vélib' (www.velib.paris.fr), also introduced to the city's outskirts. Nobody could have predicted how quickly Île-de-France residents would take to their bikes, even though cycle routes have been expanding for years (Paris now has 371km of them). Vélib' is actually very easy to use if you're thinking of hiring a bike for the day (see p159 for more information). If you have your own bike, don't forget that you can take it on RER lines. Vélib' has been so successful that a similar scheme is being considered, called Autolib', which will offer 2,000 electric cars for hire in Paris and another 2000 that can be picked up in the suburbs.

Another transport innovation is the boat shuttle Voguéo (www.vogueo.fr; tickets €3; 🕓 7am-8.30pm, every 20 min weekdays, every 30 min weekends), linking the Gare d'Austerlitz train station to Maisons-Alfort, stopping at the Bibliothèque Nationale de France (p 77), Bercy (p 77) and the Port d'Ivry.

Trams (www.tramway.paris.fr) have also made their comeback in the south of Paris with the T2 and T3 lines running through the suburbs. Work is in progress to extend the route to the northeast of Paris and should be finished by 2012.

Hermé's famous macaroons (p70)

>9 THE NEW GOURMET PARIS

'Bistronomie' is the only word on the lips of every food-lover in Paris at the moment. And no wonder: bistronomy is perhaps best described as being the equivalent of gastropub food: modern food which is simple and low-key, yet innovative. It doesn't involve elaborate service in an imposing restaurant; you'll find it being served in lively, down-to-earth venues. Yves Camdebord's food was the first to be described admiringly as bistronomique. Today you can find this chef creating mouth-watering dishes at Le Comptoir (p72). The young Basque chef, Inaki Aizpitarte, who learned his trade at La Famille (p126), has now opened Le Chateaubriand (p111). To try this new concept for yourself, you can also head to L'Ami Jean (p73), Le Pré Verre (p72) or the Symples de l'Os à Moëlle (p71). *Le Fooding®* (www.lefooding.com), a restaurant guide, suggests other venues offering creative dishes in an enjoyable and relaxed atmosphere, free from the constraints of the usual stuffy restaurant traditions.

Parisians love going to the city's markets (the Market d'Aligre has a particularly devoted following, p92), to buy utensils from designer shops or cook-books from specialist bookshops like La Cocotte (www.lacocotte .net), and to take cookery courses from chefs in workshops such as L'Academie Cinq Sens (www.academiecinqsens.com). Even the Ritz (www.ritz escoffier.fr) is jumping on the cookery-class bandwagon! Another great place to take lessons is L'Atelier de Fred (www.latelierdefred.com) in Le Marais.

Painted mural, Butte-aux-Cailles (p73)

>10 STREET ART

Even the walls form part of this city's art scene. Apart from publicly commissioned art such as the metro installation of Jean-Michel Othoniel on Place Colette and Buren at the Palais-Royal, which had its columns renovated and was given a second official opening in January 2010, you'll spot graffiti, stickers and other street art around the city, especially in Belleville, Ménilmontant, Montmartre and the Butte-aux-Cailles.

The Space Invaders (www.space-invaders.com) who 'invade' cities with little signature mosaics, have left their mark on Paris. Artists like Miss Tic (www.misticinparis.com) with her stencil art and witty aphorisms, Jérôme Mesnager (http://mesnagerjerome.free.fr) and his white stencilled male figures, and André's cheeky Mr A, have gained widespread recognition. Miss Tic now also exhibits her work in Éric Landau's Galerie W (44 Rue Lepic, 18th), Mesnager has created a huge fresco on Rue de Ménilmontant (p108), while André runs the Black Block store at the Palais de Tokyo (p44) and co-owns the trendy club Le Baron (p51).

On the corner of Rue Saint-Maur and Rue Oberkampf, a wall regularly displays work by artists from the Association Le MUR (http://lemurasso.fr). You'll also spot walls painted by Aki Kuroda (15-17 Rue du Colonel Driant, 1st), Pierre Alechinsky (38 Rue Descartes, 5th), Yvaral (105 Rue du Faubourg-Saint-Denis, 10th), Jan Voss (Rue de Metz, 10th), Jean-Charles Blais (58 Rue Damesme, 13th), Jacques de la Villeglé (5 Rue Baudricourt, 13th) and an impressive creation by Ben, Marie Bourget, Jean Le Gac and JM Albert (52 Rue de Belleville, 20th).

Parc André Citroën

>11 PARIS FOR FAMILIES

Paris isn't just for adults. There is even a café for under-16s on the Canal de l'Ourcq: Le Cafézoïde has games, shows and cosy corners for gossiping (☎ 01 42 38 26 37; www.cafezoide.asso.fr; 92 bis Quai de la Loire; ☺ 10am-7pm Wed-Sun), while the Les 400 Coups restaurant (☎ 01 40 40 77 78; www .les400coups.eu; 12 bis rue de la Villette; 10.30am-6pm Wed-Sun, to 9pm Sat; Ⓜ Jourdain) was designed by two mothers especially for parents of young children.

Disneyland Paris (www.disneylandparis.com), the world's largest theme park, the Jardin du Luxembourg, which offers pony rides and playground areas, and the Jardin d'Acclimatation (www.jardindacclimatation.fr) in the Bois de Boulogne with its rides, shows and workshops are all classic venues that will appeal to kids. In Paris, the Musée en Herbe (☎ 01 40 67 97 66; www.musee-en-herbe.com; 21 Rue Herold, 1st), holds art workshops for children (from 30 months), as well as exhibitions designed for children and visits in foreign languages.

The Louvre and Musée d'Orsay offer workshops and themed tours, the Palais de Tokyo (p44) puts on Tok Tok workshops for children aged five to 10, the Cité de la Musique (p134) and the Musée du quai Branly (p44) provide tours with stories, while the Pompidou Centre (p29) has a children's gallery with specially designed exhibitions and is soon to have one for teenagers. The Cité des Enfants de la Villette (p135), the children's gallery at the Grande Galerie de l'Évolution at the Natural History Museum (☎ 01 40 79 54 79; www.mnhn.fr; 36 Rue Geoffroy-Saint-Hilaire, 5th) and the Trocadéro Cinéaqua aquarium (☎ 01 40 69 23 23; www.cineaqua.com; 5 Av Albert-de-Mun, 16th) are also popular with both older and younger visitors. Meanwhile, the Canal de l'Ourcq is a great place to go rollerblading or cycling. Those who like sport will also enjoy a visit to the Stade de France (p120), while those who prefer planes should head to the Musée de l'Air et de l'Espace in Le Bourget (p147).

Paris, a city full of expression

>12 PARIS ON STAGE

Performing arts in Paris can't be restricted to one venue or one association. Dance performances can be seen at places such as the Théâtre de la Ville (☎ 01 42 74 22 77; www.theatredelaville-paris.com; 2 Pl du Châtelet, 4th), the Centre National de la Danse in Pantin (p136), the Théâtre National de Chaillot (☎ 01 53 65 30 00; www.theatre-chaillot.fr; 3 Pl du Trocadéro, 16th) and the Ménagerie de Verre (☎ 01 43 38 33 44; www.menagerie-de-verre.org; 12-14 Rue Léchevin, 11th).

Along with their avant-garde stage ensembles, stage directors Ariane Mnouchkine and Bartabas have literally invented places like La Cartoucherie where Mnouchkine is resident (☎ 01 43 74 24 08; www.theatre-du-soleil.fr; Route Champ de Manœuvres, 12th) and stages popular, high-quality productions, and Zingaro (☎ 01 48 39 18 03; www.theatre-zingaro.com; 176 Av Jean-Jaurès, Aubervilliers), an equestrian theatre where Bartabas calls the shots. Suburban theatres also play a significant role, such as the MC 93 (☎ 01 41 60 72 72; www.mc93.com; 1 Bd Lénine) in Bobigny, the Théâtre des Amandiers (☎ 01 46 14 70 00; www.nanterre-amandiers.com; 7 Av. Pablo Picasso) in Nanterre, the Théâtre de la Commune (☎ 01 48 33 16 16; www.theatredelacommune.com; 2 Rue Édouard Poisson) in Aubervilliers and the Théâtre de Gennevilliers (☎ 01 41 32 26 26; www.theatre2gennevilliers.com; 41 Av. des Grésillons).

In the centre of Paris, look out for the Bouffes du Nord (☎ 01 46 07 73 73; www.bouffesdunord.com; 37 bis Bd de la Chapelle, 10th), the Théâtre de l'Odéon and the Ateliers Berthier (☎ 01 44 85 40 40; www.theatre-odeon.fr; 2 Rue Corneille, 6th), not to mention the Théâtre du Rond-Point (☎ 01 44 95 98 21; www.theatredurondpoint.fr; 2 bis Av F. Roosevelt, 8th), the Théâtre de la Colline (☎ 01 44 62 52 52; www.colline.fr; 15 Rue Malte-Brun, 20th), the Théâtre de l'Est Parisien (☎ 01 40 31 20 96; www.theatre-estparisien.net; 159 Av Gambetta, 20th) where you can often see shows in original version with subtitles, and Le Tarmac (☎ 01 40 03 93; www.letarmac.fr; Parc de la Villette). Experience the best in circus arts at the Chapiteau de la Villette big top (www.villette.com) or at the Académie Fratellini (☎ 0825 250 735; www.academie-fratellini.com; Saint-Denis-la Plaine).

PRIX DES CORNETS

GLACES BERTHILLON

VENTE
EN
CORNETS
DE GLAC
BERT LO

SPECL
DI
TARTES
SAL
A TOUTE

Map of the neighbourhoods on the inside cover

>LES HALLES AND THE LOUVRE IN FULL SWING

For those in any doubt of the Louvre's contemporary credentials, fear not – the largest museum in the world is refusing to rest on its laurels and in this sense, reflects the neighbourhood around it. In Ieoh Ming Pei's famous pyramid within the Louvre, itself a work of modern art, visitors can gaze on contemporary pieces in temporary and permanent exhibitions.

The über-stylish boutique Colette has set up shop in the neighbourhood on the Rue Saint-Honoré and has yet to meet its match. This is a place where art and fashion come together – a fact not lost on the powers within the Musée des Arts Décoratifs which has recently undergone a welcome facelift.

With the regeneration of Les Halles, city planners are seeking to continue a long string of architectural wonders including the Tuileries, the Louvre, the Palais Royal and Beaubourg, in the hope of raising the area to the stature of its prestigious neighbours. This is the nerve centre of Paris which sees thousands of people from the surrounding areas in transit every day in the underground station complex. Outside, just a few metres away, people go looking for the Parisian eating experience *à l'ancienne* in the Rue Montorgueil, a pedestrianised street packed with café terraces and eateries. Even here, the latest trends are never far away. Just watch the passers-by.

LES HALLES AND THE LOUVRE

See map on following pages

The forecourt of the Pompidou Centre – constantly abuzz with activity

SEE

POMPIDOU CENTRE

☎ 01 44 78 12 33; www.centrepompidou.fr;
Place Georges-Pompidou; museum and
exhibitions: full price/concs €10-12/8-9;
🕑 11am-9pm Wed-Mon, to 11pm Thu;
Ⓜ Rambuteau; ♿

Located within the Pompidou Centre,
the Musée National d'Art Moderne
is synonymous with contemporary
art. It displays works from all different
disciplines, offering insights into
painting, architecture and design.
In its collection of 50,000 works, you
will find fauvist, cubist, surrealist and
pop-art compositions along with
contemporary pieces. The Espace 315
also exhibits the very latest offerings
from young talents such as Claude

Closky and Urs Fischer. Exhibitions
of work from 20th-century masters,
such as Kandinsky and Calder, and
contemporary artists, like Louise
Bourgeois and Pierre Soulages, are
always very popular with visitors.
Outside in the forecourt, street artists
provide the entertainment. Enjoy
spectacular views from Le Georges
restaurant (p38).

MUSÉE DES ARTS DÉCORATIFS

☎ 01 44 55 57 50; www.lesarts
decoratifs.fr; 107 Rue de Rivoli; full
price/concs/under 18yrs €9/7.50/free;
🕑 11am-6pm Tue-Fri, 10am-6pm Sat &
Sun, to 9pm Thu; Ⓜ Palais Royal–Musée
du Louvre; ♿

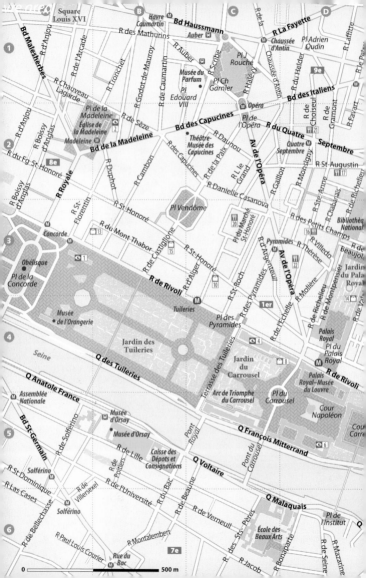

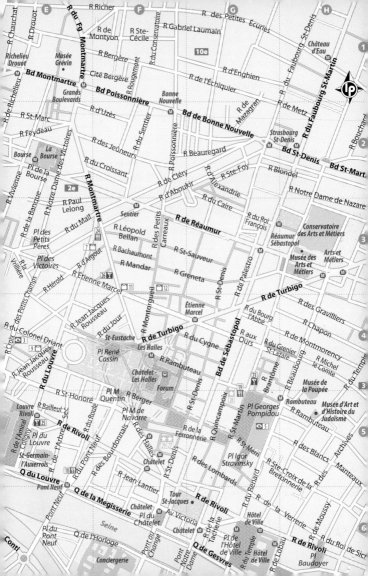

A FACELIFT FOR LES HALLES

Les Halles is set to embark on a new chapter of its history in 2013 with the completion of a project overseen by architects Patrick Berger and Jacques Anziutti who were chosen to redesign facilities dating back to the 1970s and 1980s. The Forum des Halles will be covered by a curved sheet of translucent glass, providing an abundance of natural light. The project was christened 'Canopée' by its designers in reference to the natural roof formed by the canopy of leaves in tropical rainforests. It is part of an overall strategy whereby the park will also be transformed into a single, unenclosed space.

Fresh from its recent renovations, the Musée des Arts Décoratifs, situated in one of the wings of the Louvre, now has new displays, inside and out. The new museum catalogue guides you through a collection of 150,000 items reflecting the expertise of craftsmen and manufacturers including cabinet makers, ceramists and glassworkers. Themed galleries flesh out the chronological tour from the Middle Ages to the present day. Fashion and textiles as well as advertising are among the themes of the major exhibitions which never fail to draw in the crowds, as seen with the recent retrospectives on Sonia Rykiel, Valentino or Madeleine Vionnet.

JEU DE PAUME

☎ 01 47 03 12 50; www.jeudepaume.org; 1 Place de la Concorde; full price/concs €7/5; 🕙 12pm-9pm Tue, noon-7pm Wed-Fri, 10am-7pm Sat & Sun; Ⓜ Concorde
In the northwest corner of the Jardin des Tuileries, opposite the Musée de l'Orangerie, this former tennis hall is a renowned centre for images and

photography from the 19th century to the present day. All forms of photography (including Martin Parr, Richard Avedon and Edward Steich), images and videos can be seen at exhibitions and events.

LA PINACOTHÈQUE

☎ 01 42 68 02 01; www.pinacotheque .com; 28 Place de la Madeleine; full price/concs/under 12yrs €10/8/ free; 🕙 10.30am-6pm, to 9pm Wed; Ⓜ Madeleine
The privately owned Pinacothèque de Paris christened its new space in an elegant building in the chic Madeleine district with an exhibition featuring the work of Roy Lichtenstein, one of the major luminaries of American pop art. This set the tone for off-the-wall exhibitions on original themes, exploring both contemporary work and archaeological finds. Recent exhibitions such as *The Soldiers of Eternity*, *Edvard Munch* or *l'Anti-cri* have confirmed this.

Maria Rodrigues,
Programme coordinator at Le Baiser Salé

You have been the firefly of Le Baiser Salé since it opened. What makes a place like this stand out in Paris? Le Baiser Salé keeps up the jazz-club tradition, with musicians playing three one-hour sets. We also have good acoustics, a small room where the audience feels really close to the musicians and a bar where it's easy to get chatting! However, the *quartier* also plays a role, with its open outlook and mix of cultures, reflected in our programming, which draws from many cultural sources. **Which musicians have made an impression recently?** Blick Bassy, a Cameroon singer who comes to jam from time to time and the saxophonist Guillaume Perret for his originality, even if his jazz punk is not really my thing. **The Rue des Lombards is the only street in Paris with three jazz clubs.** It's true, and they get on well! Le Baiser Salé, Le Sunset-Sunside (p40) and Le Duc des Lombards (p19) have established the Paris Jazz Club association to promote this style of music and offer a packed programme of concerts, just as London or New York have done for years. **Do you have any other favourite venues?** The New Morning (p62), of course, but also the Bataclan for concerts (p19). Apart from that, I love the brunch at La Bellevilloise (p114).

Le Baiser Salé (☎ 01 42 33 37 71; 58 Rue des Lombards, 1st; ☯ 5pm-6am; Ⓜ Châtelet)

ⓒ LE LABORATOIRE

☎ 01 78 09 49 50; www.lelaboratoire
.org; 4 Rue du Bouloi; full price/concs/
under 13 yrs €6/4.50/free; ☉ noon-7pm
Fri-Mon; Ⓜ Palais Royal–Musée du
Louvre or Louvre-Rivoli; ♿

This is a funny kind of laboratory set
up by David Edwards, a professor
at Harvard University, who wanted
to create a meeting place for artists
and scientists. Innovations and
experiments in culture, humanity
and design have emerged from
these partnerships which are
dressed up and shown to the public
in a post-industrial space covering
1300m^2. A project involving top chef
Thierry Marx and physician Jérôme
Bibette, for instance, led to the
creation of flavour capsules
for an exhibition where visitors
were invited to take part in
'experimental tastings'.

🛍 SHOP

The Les Halles and Louvre
neighbourhoods boast a number
of popular shopping areas, with the
major international chains mainly
to be found on the Rue de Rivoli
and the top brands on the Rue
Saint-Honoré. There is also a good
selection of shops on the Rue du
Jour, the top of the Rue Montmartre,
the Rue Tiquetonne and the Rue
Étienne-Marcel, while Les Halles
is home to the biggest shopping
centre in the capital.

🛍 COLETTE *Concept Store*

☎ 01 55 35 33 90; www.colette.fr;
213 Rue Saint-Honoré; ☉ 11am-7pm
Mon-Sat; Ⓜ Tuileries

Colette has been setting the trend
now for more than 10 years. The
ground floor is home to all things
hi-tech, books, music and beauty
products, while the 1st floor is a
mecca for men's and women's
fashion. There are exhibitions on the
mezzanine level and a wi-fi-enabled
water bar in the basement, serving
around 100 brands of mineral water
from across the world. Even the
window displays are artistically
decorated. Is this cool or what?

107 Rivoli, stylish shop in the Musée des Arts Décoratifs

FOR YOUR EYES ONLY

The three famous shoe designers Christian Louboutin, Pierre Hardy and Rodolphe Menudier all have boutiques in the 1st arrondissement. **Pierre Hardy** (☎ 01 42 60 59 75; www .pierrehardy.com; 156 Galerie de Valois), whose clients include Hermès and Balenciaga, has opened up shop in the narrow streets around the Palais-Royal. His highly contemporary boutique is a kind of 'black box' with waxed lino floors and ceilings all in black. **Christian Louboutin** (☎ 01 42 36 53 66; www.christianlouboutin.com; 19 Rue Jean-Jacques-Rousseau), whose shoes are instantly recognisable by their red soles, exhibits his works as if they were in an art gallery. Both Madonna and David Lynch have fallen for his charms, and Lynch even photographed his shoes for an exhibition at the Cartier Foundation. Finally, **Rodolphe Menudier** (☎ 01 42 36 86 27; www.rodolphemenudier.com; 14 Rue de Castiglione) commissioned designer Christophe Pillet to create his elegant boutique, bristling with rock 'n' roll attitude. It goes without saying that not all items are within everyone's budget but it's a good opportunity to check out quality workmanship presented in beautiful boxes.

🛍 MARIA LUISA *Fashion*
☎ 01 47 03 96 15; 2 Rue Cambon;
🕑 10.30am-7pm Mon-Sat;
Ⓜ Concorde

Like Colette but a lot more select, Maria Luisa is a fashion hub attracting those in the know. Jot down the address or even drop in, even if you're unlikely to buy anything here. Stylists reign supreme in the new boutique on Rue Rouget de l'Isle, which is a one-stop-shop for women's prêt-a-porter and accessories, replacing the outlets on the Rue Cambon and the Rue Mont-Thabor.

🛍 107 RIVOLI *Art and Design*
☎ 01 42 60 64 94; 107 Rue de Rivoli;
🕑 10am-7pm; Ⓜ Palais Royal–Musée du Louvre

The shop in the Musée des Arts Décoratifs sells a fine selection of specialist works, jewellery, stationery, tableware and toys. It's a veritable goldmine for gift ideas at affordable prices.

🛍 APPLE STORE
High-tech
☎ 01 43 16 78 00; www.apple.com;
99 Rue de Rivoli; 🕑 10am-8pm Mon-Sun;
Ⓜ Palais Royal–Musée du Louvre

The two-level Apple Store Carrousel du Louvre is located within Pei's inverted glass pyramid. A stream of young geniuses are on hand to explain the basics of the latest high-tech products. Bookings can be made for customised shopping.

🏠 KILIWATCH *Fashion*
☎ 01 42 21 17 37; www.kiliwatch.fr; 64 Rue Tiquetonne; ⏰ 2-7pm Mon, 11am-7.30pm Tue-Sat; Ⓜ Étienne-Marcel

With its laid-back vibe, this former second-hand clothes shop is a must for original streetwear including trainers, sunglasses, bags…and believe it or not, there is still a wide selection of second-hand clothes. There is also an OFR bookshop in a corner space specialising in photography and graphic art. A great place to go shopping for jeans.

🏠 KOKON TO ZAI *Fashion*
☎ 01 42 36 92 41; 48 Rue Tiquetonne; ⏰ 11.30am-7.30pm Mon-Sat; Ⓜ Étienne-Marcel or Les Halles

This long and narrow space which mixes a techno vibe with London chic is a haven for avant-garde fashion by designers such as Marjan Pejoski, Jeremy Scott and Bernhard Willhelm.

🏠 ALMOST FAMOUS *Fashion*
☎ 01 40 41 05 21; 65 Rue d'Argout; ⏰ 2-7.30pm Mon, 11.30am-7.30pm Tue-Sat; Ⓜ Sentier

This small boutique opened by designer David Hermelin sells items from Hermelin's own collections as well as a variety of other designer labels including Isabel Marant, Bruuns Bazaar and See by Chloé at reasonable prices. The pioneering house label, Almost Famous

Rue Montorgueil, a perfect balance between traditional Paris and Paris *à la mode*

MONTORGUEIL – THE PLACE TO BE

In days gone by, the marketplace in Les Halles spilled out northwards into the cobbled street known as the Rue Montorgueil. Now pedestrianised, it crosses the Rue Étienne-Marcel, with its boutiques that are run by young fashion designers, and merges into the Rue des Petits-Carreaux.

Every day (except Monday), grocers and shopkeepers from the Rue Montorgueil set up stalls in the street offering appetising fresh produce, and both day and night, the cafés and restaurants overflow with people enjoying themselves.

While you are visiting the area, be sure to pop into the **Rocher de Cancale** (☎ 01 42 33 50 29; www.aurocherdecancale.fr; 78 Rue Montorgueil; ⏰ 8am-2am), a bistro that was once frequented by Balzac, or **Little Italy** (☎ 01 42 36 36 25; 92 Rue Montorgueil), Paris' lively answer to the famous New York trattoria which draws a trendy crowd.

Imported, focuses on offerings from young Japanese designers. A source of good ideas.

🍴 EAT

You don't have to wander far from the Louvre to find great places to eat. It's just one step away from the lively Montorgueil district which has so much to tempt the palate (see the boxed text, above). On sunny days, sitting at an outdoor table of one of the pleasant terraces situated on the Place du Marché Saint-Honoré is a real treat.

🍴 LE PETIT MARCEL

French €€

☎ 01 48 87 10 20; 65 Rue Rambuteau; ⏰ 11am-midnight; Ⓜ Rambuteau

Situated just a stone's throw from the Pompidou Centre, this bistro has something of an old-world feel with its earthenware crockery and waiters dressed in tails. However, the trendy clientele and menu bring you back to the present day, with snacks such as toasties with bread from the Poilâne bakery for small appetites and generous daily mains if you're feeling hungry.

🍴 SHAKE EAT

French €€

☎ 01 40 07 90 64; www.shake-eat.fr; 17 Rue de Choiseul; ⏰ lunch & dinner Mon-Fri, dinner only Sat; Ⓜ Quatre-Septembre

With its citrus-coloured décor, simple, Zen furnishings, delicious food inspired by Asia and Italy and a smoothie bar where they customise the drinks to taste…this place focuses on freshness and balance. Highly popular with those wanting to stay in shape…as well as with those who want to stay slim!

🍴 KONG *French, Japanese* €€€
☎ 01 40 39 09 00; www.kong.fr;
1 Rue du Pont Neuf; Ⓜ Pont Neuf
The Kong is a trendy restaurant
worth lingering in. The décor is the
first thing to seize your attention,
with all its glass panels. Designer
Philippe Starck skilfully manipulates
classical notions of a geisha to
develop a modern icon, applying
the same concept to the furniture.
Then there is the spectacular view
of the Seine (the Kong is on the top
floor of the Kenzo building). The
food is also high in quality, with
influences from Asia and elsewhere.
Brunch served on Sundays is a real
treat.

🍴 LE SAUT DU LOUP
French €€€
☎ 01 42 25 49 55; www.lesautduloup
.com; **107 Rue de Rivoli;** Ⓜ Palais Royal–
Musée du Louvre
On fine days, the restaurant located
in the Musée des Arts Décoratifs
opens its terrace in the Jardin du
Carrousel, drawing sunlovers.
The designer interior is a study in
black and white. Not particularly
adventurous, the food is still
contemporary and tasty.

🍴 GEORGES
International €€€
☎ 01 44 78 47 99; **Pompidou Centre,
Level 6, Place Georges-Pompidou;**
⏲ Wed-Mon 12pm-2am; Ⓜ Rambuteau

LITTLE TOKYO IN THE RUE SAINTE-ANNE
This street is a little slice of Japan in Paris,
with wall-to-wall Japanese restaurants
from the Avenue de l'Opéra to the Rue
Saint Augustin. It is definitely a nice
change of scenery and you can be sure
to eat well without spending too much
money. The only problem is choosing
where to go. A few suggestions: the
classic noodle bar **Higuma** (☎ 01
47 03 38 59; 32 bis Rue Sainte-Anne)
where you can see the chefs at work
and **Yasube** (☎ 01 47 03 96 37;
9 Rue Sainte-Anne ; ⏲ Mon-Sat),
slightly more expensive but delicious
with a large basement room where
diners follow the age-old tradition of
sitting on the floor to eat. Not far from
here, make sure you take a look at the
quality Japanese supermarket **Issé et
Cie** (☎ 01 42 96 26 74; 11 Rue Saint-
Augustin; ⏲ 11am-7.30pm) offering
a wide range of products, most of which
can be tasted before buying. Cookery
classes are also organised here.

As well as aluminium caverns and
polar-white seats, this industrial-
looking restaurant located on the
6th floor of the Pompidou Centre
offers a stunning view across the
Paris rooftops from its terrace.
A unique backdrop for a post-
exhibition drink.

La Fusée, tucked away near the Pompidou Centre

DRINK

Make a bee-line for the Montorgueil district which is bursting at the seams with bars and cafés.

LE TAMBOUR *Bar*
☎ 01 42 33 06 90; 41 Rue Montmartre; Ⓜ Étienne-Marcel or Sentier
This is a refuge for night owls and/or insomniacs who are greeted with a friendly din and 100% Parisian décor that has been salvaged from the city's public transport system, not to mention generous helpings of French cuisine for less than €20 served until 3.30 am.

LE CAFÉ NOIR *Bar*
☎ 01 40 39 07 36; 65 Rue Montmartre; ◷ 8am-2am Mon-Fri, 4pm-2am Sat; Ⓜ Sentier
Day and night, this café is abuzz with the conversations of punters perched on the red moleskin stools or crowded around the small zinc counter. This is trendiness at its mostest, although you'll find it's a touch more rock 'n' roll than some other places.

LE FUMOIR *Bar*
☎ 01 42 92 00 24; 6 Rue de l'Amiral-de-Coligny; ◷ 11am-2am; Ⓜ Louvre-Rivoli
These days, the *fumoir* (smoking room) is the great outdoors due to the smoking ban in indoor public areas, but the place has lost none of its charm. Both chic and cosy, attracting a well-heeled, trendy crowd for a drink from the superb cocktail menu or a meal. During the day, the atmosphere is more laid-back (reading material available).

LA FUSÉE *Café*
☎ 01 42 76 93 99; 168 Rue Saint-Martin; ◷ 10am-2am; Ⓜ Rambuteau
Situated a mere stone's throw away from the Pompidou Centre, but set apart from the crowds, this lively café is as trendy as it is colourful. Great for a late breakfast, daytime snack or late-evening drink.

Le Café Noir (p39) – a stylish bar with zany décor

⭐ PLAY

Jazz lovers should make straight for the Rue des Lombards, a quiet street between Les Halles and the Pompidou Centre, which features three mythical Parisian jazz-clubs, namely Le Baiser Salé (see p33), Le Sunset-Sunside and Le Duc des Lombards. Every two months, these clubs put on special *Paris Jazz Club* evenings (www.parisjazzclub.net).

⭐ SUNSET-SUNSIDE
Jazz Venue

☎ 01 40 26 46 60; www.sunset-sunside .com; 60 Rue des Lombards; entry free-

€25; ⏱ concerts 8pm; Ⓜ Châtelet
The greatest jazz musicians have played the small cavern room in the Sunset, a jazz hotspot which doubled in size several years ago when the Sunside club opened. Since then, there has been a clear division between electric jazz, electro-jazz and world music played at the Sunset and acoustic jazz at the Sunside. Two concerts are held every evening and both the jazz greats (including Kenny Barron, Kurt Elling and Terry Callier) and new talent, such as Erik Truffaz and Julien Lourau, never pass up the opportunity to play here.

⭐ LE TROISIÈME LIEU
Club

☎ 01 48 04 85 64; 62 Rue Quincampoix; free entry; ⏱ 6pm-2am Mon-Sat; Ⓜ Rambuteau
Like its owners, the 'Ginettes Armées' lesbian collective, this bar is laid-back with a party feel. Diners sit at large tables (excellent *tartines* and plates of *charcuterie*) and people dance at the bar (if not on the tables) or in the submarine, a strange little basement room. There is also a caravan with DJ sets on Wednesday to Saturday. Branching out with a record shop My Electro Kitchen, the Ginettes also organise a host of events.

> A NEW LOOK AT THE CHAMPS-ÉLYSÉES AND WESTERN PARIS

The Eiffel Tower, the Arc de Triomphe and the Champs-Élysées are all very impressive, but there is more to the west of Paris than this opulence and grandeur. Contemporary design has also made its mark, embodied by the view of the Grande Arche de la Défense. Modernity is even evident on the Avenue des Champs-Élysées itself, where car showrooms compete with imaginative flair and Citroën's three-dimensional glass façade bearing the double-chevron logo dazzles, as do the luxury brands that call the Avenue home (the opening of the Louis Vuitton boutique created a major stir).

Centres of exhibition mirror this ostentation and are often imposing (the Palais de Tokyo, Musée du quai Branly and the Nave of the Grand Palais, for example), although some are more low-key with luxury and discretion their watchwords. The neighbourhood is a chic evening destination where visitors revel in the history steeped in former bordellos and boathouses or the stylish comfort of hotel bars. This is definitely the place to see and be seen.

CHAMPS-ÉLYSÉES AND WESTERN PARIS

See map on following pages

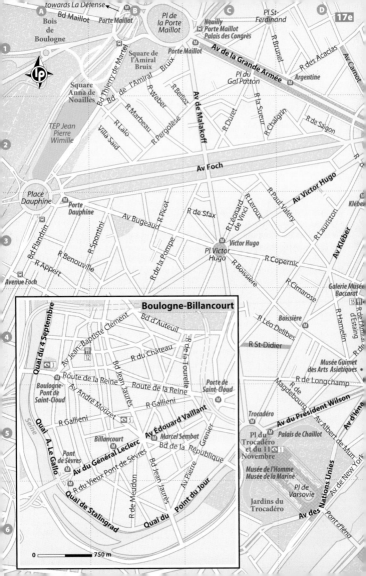

THE CHAMPS-ÉLYSÉES AND WESTERN PARIS

👁 SEE

The Grande Arche de la Défense, which is visible when looking down the Champs-Élysées from the Arc de Triomphe, is a stark reminder: however historic the district is, it is in a state of constant development. The numerous attractions on the periphery of the major monuments bear testament to this.

👁 PALAIS DE TOKYO

☎ 01 47 23 54 01; www.palaisdetokyo.com; 13 Av du Président Wilson; full price/concs €6/4.50, admission plus *plat du jour* & coffee €15; ⏲ noon-midnight Tue-Sun; Ⓜ Iéna or RER C Pont de l'Alma; ♿

There is always something going on at the Palais de Tokyo, the only museum in Paris open until midnight. Instead of a permanent collection, the museum organises a series of temporary exhibitions which demystify French and international contemporary art in all its forms, including photography and video. The artists occasionally curate exhibitions and the Pavillon hosts young artists in residence. There's also something for the kids with the Tok Tok workshops organised in age groups from three to 10 years old. This steel and concrete structure is also home to a restaurant (p49), a cafeteria, a bookshop and the BlackBlock museum store directed by graffiti artist André, a place to find weird and wonderful objects.

The stylish and cool Palais de Tokyo cafeteria

👁 MUSÉE DU QUAI BRANLY

☎ 01 56 61 70 00; www.quaibranly.fr; 37 Quai Branly; admission full price/concs €8.50/6, temporary exhibitions €7/5, combined ticket €13/9.50; ⏲ 11am-7pm Tues, Wed and Sun, to 9pm Thu-Sat; closed Mon; Ⓜ Alma Marceau, Iéna or Bir-Hakeim, or RER C Pont de l'Alma; ♿

There is a permanent display of nearly 4000 objects here, from Africa, Oceania, Asia and the Americas. The museum also features major exhibitions, such as the recent *Teotihuacan, The Minghei Spirit in*

LA DÉFENSE FOCUSES ON ARCHITECTURE

The La Défense neighbourhood is undergoing a revival. At the forefront of this is the new Tour Signal, which is to be built close to the Grande Arche (project put on hold) following Jean Nouvel's winning design. Conceived by the architect as a great tower symbolising the regeneration of La Défense, the skyscraper, designed with sustainable development in mind, will be 301m high, have 71 floors and consist of offices, businesses, residential flats and a hotel.

A flagship, emblematic monument for the business district characterised by its futuristic glass and chrome towers, the **Grande Arche** (☎ 01 49 07 27 27; www.grandearche .com; 1 Parvis de la Défense; full price/concs €10/8.50; ⌚ 10am-8pm Apr-Aug, to 7pm Sep-Mar; Ⓜ La Défense–Grande Arche) is situated in the historic axis of Paris, formed by the Arc de Triomphe and the Louvre (note the precise alignment of the three arches). This perfect cube made of white Carrara marble and grey granite was designed by Danish architect Johan Otto von Spreckelsen. A glass elevator transports you 110m skyward to the **roof of the** Grande Arche, which houses the Musée de l'Informatique, a terrace with a view over the great axis and the restaurant Ô 110, a brasserie and cybercafé. Over 70 contemporary sculptures can be seen in various locations all over the *quartier*, including those by the well-known artists Miró, Calder, César or Moretti.

Architecture buffs will enjoy the **Musée de la Défense** (☎ 01 47 74 84 24; www.ladefense .fr; 15 Place de la Défense; free entry; ⌚ 10am-6pm, to 7pm on Sat; Ⓜ La Défense–Grande Arche) and its collection of drawings, plans and models, as well as projects that never came to fruition. At the same location, the information centre provides a map of the area with architectural routes marked out.

Japan and *The Artics*. The Musée du quai Branly was designed by the architect Jean Nouvel. The exhibition hall, which follows the curve of the Seine, rests 10m above the ground on columns that look like tree trunks, positioned in the garden designed by Gilles Clément, seemingly at random to reflect the vagaries of nature. Inside, the atmosphere is softened by a long stained-glass window, which filters the natural light, while outside a stunning living wall by Patrick Blanc adorns the façade, studded with 'boxes' of different colours and sizes.

The restaurant **Les Ombres** (☎ 01 47 53 68 00; www.lesombres-restaurant.com) offers an unobstructed view of the Eiffel Tower.

◖ MUSÉE D'ART MODERNE DE LA VILLE DE PARIS

☎ 01 53 67 40 00; www.mam.paris.fr; 11 Av du Président-Wilson; permanent collection free entry, temporary exhibitions full price/concs €5/3.50; ⌚ 10am-6pm Tues-Sun, temporary exhibitions nightly to10pm; Ⓜ léna; ♿

Near the Palais de Tokyo, the Museum of Modern Art covers almost all of the major artistic movements of the

The huge Nave of the Grand Palais hosts exhibitions

20th and the early 21st centuries: fauvism, cubism, dadaism, surrealism and abstraction are all present, with works by artists such as Picasso, Modigliani, Braque and Chagall. The MAM regularly organises ambitious exhibitions and opens its doors to contemporary artists.

◉ NAVE OF THE GRAND PALAIS

www.grandpalais.fr; Av Winston Churchill; admission varies depending on events and exhibitions; ☉ **10am-**

7pm Mon & Wed, to 10pm Thu-Sun; Ⓜ **Champs-Élysées Clemenceau or Franklin D Roosevelt;** ♿
The sheer scale of its metal-framed glass ceiling, the largest in Europe, is breathtaking. Since reopening after renovation works, the Nave has scheduled a series of high-profile events and exhibitions, many of which showcase contemporary art, such as Artparis, Fiac and Étés de la Danse. Every year, an artist creates a new work to match the scale of the venue itself for the *Monumenta* exhibition. Following on from Anselm Kiefer in 2007, Richard Serra in 2008 and Christian Boltanski in 2010, it is the turn of the Anglo-Indian artist Anish Kapoor in 2011. See p9 for the Force de l'Art.

◉ PIERRE BERGÉ–YVES SAINT-LAURENT FOUNDATION

☎ **01 44 31 64 31; www.fondation-pb-ysl.net; 3 Rue Léonce Reynaud; full price/concs €5/3;** ☉ **11am-6pm Tue-Sun, two exhibitions per year Oct–end Jan and mid-Mar–end Jul;** Ⓜ **Alma Marceau**
Until his death, Yves Saint-Laurent took a major interest in the exhibitions presented by the foundation he created with Pierre Bergé. In an intimate atmosphere, the works displayed offer an insight into the artist's world, his passion for Morocco together with other interests, such as the costumes of the last maharajas and furniture designed by Jean-Michel Franck.

LA COLLINE DES MUSÉES, CREATIVITY IN ALL ITS FORMS

Located on both sides of the Colline de Chaillot, the Cité de l'Architecture et du Patrimoine, the Musée d'Art Moderne de la Ville de Paris, the Musée du quai Branly and the Palais de Tokyo are joining forces to promote contemporary creativity. On presentation of a leaflet available at the museums, a full price admission in one of the four partner sites gives access to reduced prices to two others and free admission to the last one, whatever the order you chose to visit them in, and this is valid for five consecutive days. See www.lacollinedesmusees.com.

☉ CITÉ DE L'ARCHITECTURE ET DU PATRIMOINE

☎ 01 58 51 52 00; www.citechaillot.fr; 1 Place du Trocadéro; permanent collection or temporary exhibitions full price/concs €8/5, combined ticket €10/7; ☼ 11am-7pm Wed-Mon, to 9pm Thu; Ⓜ Trocadéro; ♿

Inside the Palais de Chaillot, the Cité (the largest architectural centre in the world) houses the *Galerie de Moulages* – or Cast Gallery – featuring life-size reproductions of the most prestigious architectural masterpieces from the 12th to the 18th century. On the upper level, the contemporary architecture gallery retraces developments in urban planning from 1850 to the current day.

Considerable space is also dedicated to current projects. The well-lit gallery follows the curve of the building and includes a reconstruction of an apartment from Le Courbusier's Cité Radieuse in Marseille. Impressive view of the Eiffel Tower from Café Carlu.

☉ ESPACE CULTUREL LOUIS VUITTON

☎ 01 53 57 52 03; www.louisvuitton .com; 60 Rue Bassano or via the boutique at 101 Av des Champs-Élysées; free entry; ☼ noon-7pm Mon-Sat, 11am-7pm Sun; Ⓜ George V; ♿

If you're planning to visit the Espace Culturel Louis Vuitton, which holds three themed exhibitions per year relating to the brand (and offers a beautiful view of Paris from the 7th floor), go through the shop! The interior, designed by Peter Marino, is a superb example of art deco. A wonderful setting for the designs of Vuitton's artistic director, Marc Jacobs.

⬗ SHOP

Despite the high rents, many brands are keen to obtain an address on the Avenue des Champs-Élysées, home to car showrooms (eg Renault and C42 Citroën), luxury brands (eg Vuitton, Cartier, Guerlain), ready-to-wear fashion brands (eg Zara, Gap), and entertainment retailers (eg Virgin, Fnac), with the latter open late (until midnight) and on Sundays.

WELCOME ESCAPE IN BOULOGNE

Boulogne-Billancourt is a pleasant surprise. 1930s islets pepper the town, which architecture enthusiasts will delight in discovering. The town hall and the post office are emblems of the style that characterised the town between the two wars (make sure you go inside if they are open). At that time Boulogne-Billancourt boasted around 30 sculptors' ateliers and the greatest artists of the time chose to live or work there, starting with Mallet-Stevens and Le Corbusier who produced their drawings in the Quartier des Princes, Allée des Pins, Rue de la Tourelle and Rue Denfert-Rochereau. The town council publishes a guide to the 1930s architecture trail known as the *Parcours des Années 30* (available from the Musée des Années 30) and offers guided walks (for information and reservations call ☎ 01 55 18 50 50; €6).

Musée des Années 30 (☎ 01 55 18 53 00; www.annees30.com; Espace Landowski, 28 Av André-Morizet; full price/concs €4.70/3.60; ☼ 11am-6pm Tue-Sun, closed 1-15 Aug; Ⓜ Marcel-Sembat). Situated alongside the town hall, in the Espace Landowski, this museum reflects the architectural and industrial history of the town. The top floor, mainly dedicated to furnishings (including a magnificent screen made of glass, mirrored glass, iron and lead) and architecture, is our favourite. You can also visit a fine collection of drawings and a room devoted to the School of Paris. The exhibition also has examples of colonial art, religious art and monumental sculpture.

Musée Albert-Kahn (☎ 01 55 19 28 00; 14 Rue du Port; full price/under 12yrs €1.50/ free; ☼ 11am-6pm Tue to Sun Oct-Apr, to 7pm May-Sep; Ⓜ Boulogne–Pont de Saint-Cloud or T2 Parc de Saint-Cloud). A banker by profession, Albert Kahn (1860–1940) devoted a large part of his life to encouraging the interaction between different cultures. His property was among the main sites where he took action. Over the four-hectare grounds, he established different gardens which still take visitors on voyages of discovery. The pleasant walk takes you from a Japanese village to an English garden, through a French garden, blue forest, rose garden, Vosges forest, and so on. The museum collections, exhibited in temporary shows, are also worth a look. From 1909 to 1931, Albert Kahn financed photographic and cinematographic campaigns all over the world. The museum now owns the world's largest collection of photographs made using autochrome plates, the first industrial colour photography process, which was first marketed in 1907.

Fish and seafood lovers should treat themselves to a jaunt to **Boulogne-sur-Mer** (☎ 01 46 04 12 87; 11 bis Av Jean-Baptiste Clément; ☼ Tue-Sat; Ⓜ Boulogne–Jean Jaurès), an establishment that has had the inspired idea of combining a fishmonger's and a restaurant. Here you can choose your fish directly from those on display.

🏠 **DRUGSTORE PUBLICIS**
Concept Store
☎ 01 44 43 75 07; www.publicis
drugstore.com; 133 Av des Champs-
Élysées; ☼ 8am-2am Mon-Fri, 10am-
2am Sat & Sun; Ⓜ Charles de Gaulle–
Étoile or George V

A true Champs-Élysées institution, the Drugstore is in no way behind the times. The attractive and welcoming space includes a brasserie (with wi-fi), a specialist food store, a pharmacy, a wine and cigar cellar, a beauty salon and a gift section. The news kiosk with its wide range of international titles is not to be missed.

🗋 LE 66 *Concept Store*
☎ 01 53 53 33 80; www.le66.fr; 66 Av des Champs-Élysées; ⏱ 11am-8pm Mon-Fri, 11.30am-8.30pm Sat, 2pm-8pm Sun; Ⓜ George V or Franklin D Roosevelt
Don't be fooled by the gloomy air of the shopping arcade that hides away this very contemporary store. Over 1200 sq metres is shared between a number of shops, with lesser-known (and therefore more accessibly priced) small designers shoulder-to-shoulder with more established international brands. In addition to fashion accessories, there is also a department selling rare DVDs and a well-stocked book section.

🍴 EAT
Picnicking is a must in this neighbourhood. The expansive lawn of the Champ-de-Mars, which extends to the foot of the Eiffel Tower, is the perfect spot to lay your picnic blanket. You can stock up on provisions at **Rue Cler** (⏱ 7am or 8am-7pm Tue-Sat, to noon Sun; Ⓜ École Militaire), which bustles with activity, especially on the weekend.

🍴 COJEAN
Sandwich Shop   €
☎ 01 45 61 07 33; www.cojean.fr; 25 Rue Washington; ⏱ 10am-4pm Mon-Fri; Ⓜ George V
A great place to enjoy a healthy lunchtime sandwich (baguettes, wraps, toasted sandwiches), salad, soup – hot or cold, depending on the season – or fruit juice during the week, in a minimalist blue space. Wi-fi and newspapers available.

🍴 TOKYO EAT
Contemporary   €€
☎ 01 47 20 00 29; www.palaisdetokyo .com; 13 Av du Président Wilson; ⏱ Tue-Sun; Ⓜ Iéna or RER C Pont de l'Alma
The Palais de Tokyo restaurant has a fashionable and arty atmosphere. The colourfully designed tables, chairs and lighting complement the Bernard Brunon mural. The menu is in keeping with this: the palate-teasing dishes never sacrifice style.

🍴 RESTAURANT DU ROND-POINT *French*   €€-€€€
☎ 01 44 95 98 44; www.restaurantdu rondpoint.fr; 2 bis Av Franklin Roosevelt; ⏱ lunch Mon-Fri, dinner Tue-Sat; Ⓜ Franklin D Roosevelt or Champs Élysées–Clemenceau
A joyous theatricality fills this restaurant, all turquoise carpet and brightly coloured walls. This is apt given its location in the Théâtre du Rond-Point. The menu features

classics (steak, risotto, cheeseburgers); for more adventurous tastes, there is the Assiette du Rond-Point or the Planche Mixte.

🍴 CAFE PLEYEL
Contemporary €€€

☎ 01 53 75 28 44; www.cafesallepleyel .com; 252 Rue du Faubourg Saint-Honoré; 🕒 lunch only; Ⓜ Ternes

The Salle Pleyel is a classical music venue that has opened up not only to rock or house music (Patti Smith, Laurent Garnier), but also to fine food! Behind the windows of the former dance studios on the upper floor, this designer-chic eating place features a red, black and white decor and each year invites a well-known chef (Sonia Ezgulian in 2010). The menu reflects the setting: original, delicious and sophisticated.

🍴 CRISTAL ROOM BACCARAT
Fine Dining €€€€

☎ 01 40 22 11 10; www.baccarat.fr; 11 Place des Etats-Unis; 🕒 Mon-Sat; Ⓜ Iéna

On the 1st floor of the Musée du Cristal Baccarat, the Cristal Room's extravagant, chic design is the work of the inimitable Philippe Starck. The space almost groans under the weight of the chandeliers. You need to book a long time ahead to sample the cuisine of Guy Martin, seconded by Thomas L'Hérisson. Enjoy the garden terrace in summer.

Chandeliers at the Cristal Room Baccarat

🍴 PIERRE GAGNAIRE
Fine Dining €€€€

☎ 01 58 36 12 50; www.pierre-gagnaire .com; 6 Rue Balzac; 🕒 lunch Mon-Fri, dinner daily; Ⓜ Charles de Gaulle–Étoile

Pierre Gagnaire breathes life into classic French cooking without succumbing to the fashion for fusion (no bubblegum ice cream here). Every dish is a visual and gastronomic work of art. The reputation of Le Grand Dessert de Pierre Gagnaire precedes it.

DRINK

MATHIS BAR *Bar*

☎ 01 53 76 01 62; 3 Rue de Ponthieu; ⏰ from 10pm Mon-Sat; Ⓜ Franklin D Roosevelt

This small bar is decorated like a deluxe boudoir. Stars treat it like a second home and as a result, it can be rather hard to get in. But it's definitely worth trying your luck.

BAR DU PLAZA ATHÉNÉE *Bar*

☎ 01 53 67 66 00; www.plaza-athenee -paris.fr; 25 Av Montaigne; ⏰ 6pm-2am; Ⓜ Alma Marceau or Franklin D Roosevelt

The blue glass bar dominates this stunning venue. With an original cocktail in hand, you can sit at the bar or in one of the comfortable leather sofas, a prime position to watch the well-heeled crowd.

PLAY

LE BARON *Club*

☎ 01 47 20 04 01; www.clublebaron .com; 6 Av Marceau; free entry; ⏰ 11pm-5am; Ⓜ Alma Marceau

This former brothel is now Paris' hippest club, frequented by all the great and the good. Reviving the fashion for small clubs, Le Baron has brought a breath of fresh air to Paris'

nightlife. A draconian door policy. Try to look like a celebrity!

MADAM *Club*

☎ 01 53 76 02 11; www.madam.fr; 128 Rue de la Boëtie; free entry; ⏰ 11pm-dawn, Fri & Sat & nights before public holidays; Ⓜ George V or Franklin D Roosevelt

Like Le Baron, Madam falls into the category of *bijou* nightclub. It does, however, have more of a house music vibe and is less selective.

LE SHOWCASE *Club*

☎ 01 45 61 25 43; www.showcase.fr; Pont Alexandre III, Port des Champs-Élysées; €12-20; ⏰ Fri & Sat 11.30pm-dawn; Ⓜ Champs-Élysées Clemenceau

This large nightclub in a former boathouse on the Pont Alexandre III draws in the crowds with its vaulted ceilings and schedule of live acts and international groups.

LE RÉGINE *Club*

☎ 01 43 59 21 13; www.leregine.com; 49 rue de Ponthieu; €10-15; ⏰ 11pm-6am Wed-Sat; Ⓜ George V

The place to be in the 1980s, revamped in 2009, this nightclub is once again in the spotlight. Techno, electronic and pop feature at this very trendy club. Occasionally open on Sunday nights.

>THE CANAL SAINT-MARTIN, AND GRANDS BOULEVARDS

Surely one of the neighbourhoods to undergo the most dramatic makeover in recent years, the Canal Saint-Martin has prompted a sea change in fashions with an endless string of hip venues springing up on its banks. It's easy to lose count of the cafés, restaurants and shops that have emerged in the wake of Chez Prune and Antoine et Lili, which are almost starting to seem a little old-hat these days if not for the hordes of new devotees who flock to them.

One trait of this trendy yet grass-roots area is the way it consciously plays with the imagery of the canal and sets new trends. The bar-restaurant Hôtel du Nord, a nod to the famous film by Marcel Carné with the impish Arletty, is a perfect example. Whilst Parisian trend-setters currently have their sights set on the east, this is by no means limited to the canal. Pockets of activity are emerging in the multicultural areas around the Gare du Nord and the Gare de l'Est and on the Grands Boulevards, which are popular haunts for nightowls. Slowly but surely, the map of trendy spots in Paris is being redrawn.

THE CANAL SAINT-MARTIN AND GRANDS BOULEVARDS

👁 SEE
Couvent des Récollets 1   F4

👜 SHOP
Antoine et Lili 2   F4
Artazart 3   F5
Aurore Capucine 4   B3
La Galerie Végétale 5   F4
Le Bazar Éthique 6   F5
Liza Korn 7   F5

🍴 EAT
Café Panique 8   D3

Ganesha Corner and
   Restaurant Ganesha 9   F1
Hôtel du Nord 10   F4
La Cantine de Quentin .. 11   F4
Le Cambodge 12   G5
Le Verre Volé 13   F4
L'Office 14   C4
Ploum 15   G5
Restaurant Dishny 16   F1

🍸 DRINK
Café A .... (See 1)
Chez Jeannette 17   D5
Chez Prune 18   G5

Delaville Café 19   C5
La Patache 20   F5
Le Jemmapes 21   G5

⭐ PLAY
Bizz'art 22   G2
Favela Chic 23   G6
Le Limonaire 24   B5
New Morning 25   D4
Point Éphémère 26   G2
Rex Club 27   C5
Social Club 28   B6

See map on following pages

SEE

The first thing that comes to most people's minds when talking about the Canal Saint-Martin is taking a stroll – the best way to discover the neighbourhood and its atmosphere, both hip and down-to-earth.

CANAL SAINT-MARTIN

Locks, latticed metal footbridges, swing bridges and tree-lined squares… this is what you can expect along this canal linking the Bassin de la Villette to the Seine, which it joins at the Port de l'Arsenal near the Bastille. There are 8 locks along the canal between La Villette and the Rue du Faubourg-du-Temple. The rest of its course then flows largely underground. Lined with shops, cafés, restaurants and a cycle path, it is a perfect place for a stroll. On sunny days, the banks of the canal are teeming with people out for a walk or enjoying a picnic. To escape the car fumes, go down on a Sunday or public holiday when only pedestrians and cyclists are permitted between 10am and 6pm in winter, and from 10am to 8pm in summer (April to September).

COUVENT DES RÉCOLLETS

Maison de l'Architecture; ☎ 01 42 09 31 81; www.maisonarchitecture-idf.org or www.ma-lereseau.org; 148 Rue du Faubourg Saint-Martin; free entry; ⏱ 11am-6pm Mon-Fri; Ⓜ Gare de l'Est

A lock being opened on the Canal Saint-Martin

In its secluded setting between the Gare de l'Est and the Canal Saint-Martin, this former convent is being given new life. Cross the cloisters to access the Maison de l'Architecture on the right-hand side. This building has been renovated and reopened by the Order of Architects for the Île-de-France region. Regular debates and conferences on architecture and the city are held in the old chapel. There is also a nice café.

SHOP

The best shops are mainly to be found around the canal on the Quai de Valmy side. Rue Beaurepaire has also become a good spot for retail therapy with green and arty

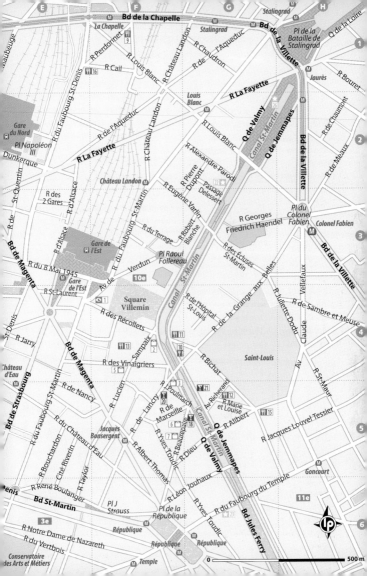

leanings. Many of the shops listed are open on Sundays.

⬜ ARTAZART *Bookshop*
☎ 01 40 40 24 00; www.artazart.com; 83 Quai de Valmy; 🕙 11am-7.30pm Mon-Sat, 1pm-7.30pm Sun; Ⓜ Jacques Bonsergent
Graphic artists, web designers and other creative types flock to this bookshop specialising in graphic arts, visual arts and other creative fields such as photography, architecture, fashion and design.

⬜ ANTOINE ET LILI
Fashion, Design
☎ clothes 01 40 37 41 55, children's wear 01 40 37 58 14, interior design wares 01 40 37 34 86; www.antoineetlili.com; 9 Quai de Valmy; 🕙 11am-8pm Tue-Sat, to 7pm Sun & Mon; Ⓜ Gare de l'Est

Something to put a smile on your face! These brightly coloured shops are part of a kind of ethno-urban village selling original garments by house designers (pink shop), pretty much the same collection for children (green shop) and flower-power interior design (yellow shop).

⬜ LA GALERIE VÉGÉTALE
Florist
☎ 01 40 37 07 16; www.lagalerievegetale.com; 29 Rue des Vinaigriers; 🕙 10.30am-7.30pm Tue-Thu, to 8pm Fri & Sat, to 7pm Sun; Ⓜ Jacques Bonsergent
Nature has taken over this impressive industrial space (an old joiner's workshop) where all forms of vegetation now hold sway. Flowers, leaves, branches and plants are presented originally for nature-themed exhibitions. There are also designer and natural products like

Antoine et Lili – dazzling window displays promise fun and colourful interiors

DEVELOPMENTS AROUND THE STATIONS

Since stations are constantly in motion, it's perhaps worth stopping a few moments to look at how they have been improved to gauge the development of a neighbourhood. Phase one of improvements to the **Gare du Nord** started with the installation of a large glass ceiling for the launch of the Eurostar and the Thalys, giving the station an injection of daylight. Since then, the surrounding area has been redeveloped to make it more user-friendly, with more space devoted to cyclists and pedestrians. In this sense, the station mirrors developments in the rest of the neighbourhood (as seen in the Boulevard Magenta). The transformation of the **Gare de l'Est** is even more striking, with both the interior and exterior undergoing major refurbishments for the opening of the new eastern TGV line. With its huge memorial painting, the station has always been very much a reminder of the suffering of the Great War. Now, however, it is a living, breathing part of people's everyday lives in the neighbourhood. It only takes a couple of minutes to get to the banks of the Canal Saint-Martin where you are in the thick of Parisian city life.

resin containers or the amazing cushions that look like stones.

🎫 LIZA KORN *Fashion*
☎ 01 42 01 36 02; www.liza-korn.com; 19 Rue Beaurepaire; ⏰ 10.30am-7.30pm Mon-Fri, 11.30am-7.30pm Sat; Ⓜ République

Designer Liza Korn was one of the first to set up shop in the neighbourhood. She is famous for her playful, rock 'n' roll fashion sensibilities and the happenings she stages to present her collections. There is now a cute collection of children's clothes and a range for the more cost-conscious.

🎫 LE BAZAR ÉTHIQUE
Fairtrade Shop
☎ 01 42 00 15 73; 25 Rue Beaurepaire; ⏰ 11am-7.30pm Tue-Sat, 2.30pm-7.30pm Sun; Ⓜ République

A fairtrade shop which proves that ethics and fashion are not mutually exclusive. Men's, women's and children's fashion, interior design and cosmetics clamour for your attention along with a specialist foods section.

🎫 AURORE CAPUCINE
Cakes, Chocolates
☎ 01 47 70 48 34; 63 Rue de Chabrol; ⏰ 8am-8pm; Ⓜ Cadet

An address for those in the know! The flower-based cakes of Aurore Capucine are still a well-kept secret. A great place to stop and buy a tasty gift before jumping on a train or catching the RER to Roissy Charles de Gaulle airport.

EAT

There is no shortage of great little places to eat in the area with

Passage Brady: a slice of India in the centre of Paris

something to offer all tastes and budgets. While trendy is the norm, décors are diverse, which avoids things getting dull.

🍽 LE CAMBODGE
Cambodian €

☎ 01 44 84 37 70; www.lecambodge.fr; 10 Av Richerand; 🕙 Mon-Sat; Ⓜ République or Goncourt

This restaurant puts on no airs and graces which is fine by us. Jot down your own order. The *bo bun* is to die for and the garnished rice dishes will convert even those most resistant to fried rice. Even if the restaurant is full (as is often the case), just leave

them your phone number and they will call you when a table frees up, giving you just enough time for a drink by the canal.

🍽 LA CANTINE DE QUENTIN
Shop, Restaurant €€

☎ 01 42 02 40 32; 52 Rue Bichat; 🕙 bistro noon-3.30pm Tue-Sun, delicatessen 10am-7.30pm; Ⓜ Gare de l'Est or Colonel Fabien

This gourmet restaurant with a burgundy façade is home to a specialist food shop and wine cellar. At lunchtimes, it opens as a bistro serving delicious traditional dishes. A few tables are set up outside when it's sunny. Brunch on Sundays.

🍽 LE VERRE VOLÉ
Wine Bar €€

☎ 01 48 03 17 34, reservations 01 48 03 17 34; www.leverrevole.fr; 67 Rue de Lancry; Ⓜ Jacques Bonsergent

This bar only has a few tables (don't forget to book!) surrounded by shelves of organic wines. It also doubles up as a wine store. There are also hearty accompaniments that come in the form of specials such as black pudding, Toulouse sausage, *andouillette* and *caillette ardéchoise* (pâté with Swiss chard). If you just want a snack, you can opt for a cheeseboard or a cold meat platter. There is another wine shop at 38 Rue Oberkampf (☎ 01 43 14 99 46).

A PASSAGE TO INDIA

There is a large Indian community in this multicultural neighbourhood. The **Passage Brady** (between 46 Rue du Faubourg Saint-Denis and 33 blvd de Strasbourg) is a classic example. Here, you will find a compact cluster of Indian, Pakistani and Bangladeshi restaurants. If you're feeling adventurous, you can go as far as the La Chapelle district between Rue Cail, Rue Louis Blanc and Rue Lafayette which is teeming with shops, Asian supermarkets and restaurants. The food, which tends to be from Sri Lanka and southern India, is authentic and therefore sometimes very spicy. Every year, between the end of August and the beginning of September, there is a procession in honour of Ganesh, one of the more benevolent Hindu gods, with thousands of people making their way to the temple on Rue Philippe de Girard.

Here are some good places to go for Indian food:

Head to the **Ganesha Corner** or the **Restaurant Ganesha** (☎ 01 58 20 07 32; 16 Rue Perdonnet, on the corner of Rue Louis-Blanc; Ⓜ La Chapelle), the former for a quick bite to eat (takeaway dishes) and the latter for a quiet lunch, or else the **Restaurant Dishny** (☎ 01 42 05 44 04; 25 Rue Cail; ☽ noon-midnight; Ⓜ La Chapelle), all reliable addresses in this *quartier*.

🍴 CAFÉ PANIQUE
French €€

☎ 01 47 70 06 84; www.cafepanique.com; **12 Rue des Messageries;** ☽ **Mon-Fri;** Ⓜ **Poissonnière or Gare du Nord**

This restaurant and gallery, invisible from the street, brings to mind an elegant loft conversion. Head chef Odile Guyader can be seen behind the kitchen counter as she concocts her experimental and sophisticated dishes at very reasonable prices.

🍴 PLOUM *Japanese* €€

☎ 01 42 00 11 90; www.ploum.fr; **20 Rue Alibert;** ☽ **lunch & dinner Mon-Fri, dinner only Sat;** Ⓜ **République or Goncourt**

Would you believe it? A Japanese restaurant that dares to be different! Set back a little way from the canal but easy to spot from the street with its huge bay window, Ploum draws a regular crowd interested in one thing – fish (both raw and cooked). For those fond of a (lot of) meat, the menu offers a large bowl of stir-fried beef with lemon grass. Besides a fine round table, the décor is fairly unadventurous.

🍴 L'OFFICE *Bistro* €€

☎ 01 47 70 67 31; **3 Rue Richer;** ☽ **lunch Thu & Fri, dinner Tue-Sat;** Ⓜ **Cadet**

Vintage wallpaper and metal lampshades… This tiny restaurant with its minimalist décor is popular with discreetly hip diners who come here to enjoy its original dishes, including Jerusalem artichoke velouté and poached-pear panacotta. The menu can be somewhat limited, but is very creative. Booking ahead is essential.

🍴 HOTEL DU NORD
Bistro €€€
☎ 01 40 40 78 78; www.hoteldunord.org; 102 Quai de Jemmapes; 🕐 restaurant noon-3pm & 8pm-midnight, café 9am-1.30am; Ⓜ Jacques Bonsergent or Colonel Fabien

A wonderful surprise! Tasty food in generous portions (raw tuna *millefeuille* with poppy seeds, pork fillet in tarragon sauce and squid-ink linguini), together with an outstanding wine list. Old-style, but elegant bistro décor. There are also a few tables outside for you to enjoy your coffee.

🍸 DRINK

Going for a drink in this area is a compulsory rite of passage. The only problem is choosing where to go. In summer, however, it's tempting to just grab the first table on offer or to sit on the banks of the canal.

🍸 CHEZ PRUNE *Bar*
☎ 01 42 41 30 47; 36 Rue Beaurepaire; 🕐 8am-2am Mon-Sat, 10am-2am Sun; Ⓜ République

Predating the surge of canal-side redevelopment, this bar-restaurant is always crawling with trendy types but it is still a place you will never tire of. Indeed why would you, with such a superb terrace overlooking the canal, which can be enjoyed on sunny days?

Delaville Café, a kitsch joint to warm up the night

🍸 DELAVILLE CAFÉ
Café
☎ 01 48 24 48 09; www.delavillecafe .com; 34 blvd Bonne Nouvelle; 🕐 11am-1.30am Mon-Sat, noon-1am Sun; Ⓜ Bonne Nouvelle

Graced with the most inviting terrace on the Grands Boulevards, the interior is also charming – a surprising blend of industrial and late 19th-century décor. The menu is seasonal but the now classic Delaville burger is a permanent fixture – full stomachs guaranteed! DJs on Wednesdays and brunch on Sundays.

🍸 LE JEMMAPES
Bar
☎ 01 40 40 02 35; 82 Quai de Jemmapes; 🕐 11am-2am; Ⓜ Jacques Bonsergent or Goncourt

Although more subdued in winter, the Jemmapes is a popular hangout when the sun comes out. People throng to the bar to grab takeaways served in plastic glasses, which they enjoy next to the canal nearby.

▼ CHEZ JEANNETTE
Bar

☎ 01 47 70 30 89; 47 Rue du Faubourg Saint-Denis; ⏱ 8am-2am; Ⓜ Strasbourg Saint-Denis

At times it doesn't take much to turn an average neighbourhood joint into a popular venue. Enter Chez Jeannette, taken over by a young team with the great idea of keeping the original décor (admittedly with a much-needed lick of paint), all mirrors, decorative mouldings, formica, wallpaper and moleskin. A happy, laid-back atmosphere.

▼ CAFÉ A *Café*

☎ 01 40 35 22 67; 148 Rue du Faubourg Saint-Martin; ⏱ 10am-8pm Tue-Fri, 2pm-10pm Sat, noon-8pm Sun May-Sept, 10am-8pm Oct-Apr; Ⓜ Gare de l'Est

A rarity indeed for Paris – a quiet setting in the shade of century-old trees in the Maison de l'Architecture (p53)! Very popular on sunny days and for Sunday brunch.

▼ LA PATACHE *Bar*

☎ 01 42 08 14 35; 60 Rue de Lancry; ⏱ 4.30pm-2am Mon-Fri, 2.30pm-2am Sat-Sun; Ⓜ Jacques Bonsergent

Mr Vito is no longer behind the bar but La Patache has a Parisian feel just the way we like it with a juke box, dark wooden bar tables and benches. Most importantly, you get a genuine smile from behind the bar. The customers are chilled out and the atmosphere, very friendly.

⭐ PLAY

This side of the Seine boasts some diverse, alternative and colourful venues for a night out. This is where the electro scene has put down its roots, especially at the Rex, but jazz and Latino rhythms also vibrate in this part of town.

⭐ POINT ÉPHEMÈRE
Live Music Venue

☎ 01 40 34 02 48; www.pointephemere .org; 200 Quai de Valmy; entry free-€15; ⏱ bar-restaurant noon-2am Mon-Sat, 1pm-9pm Sun; Ⓜ Jaurès or Louis Blanc

Housed in an old warehouse, the Point Éphémère is a burgeoning arts space with an exhibition area, bar-restaurant and music venue, hosting all kinds of gigs with styles ranging from electro and jazz to rock and funk. There are several all-night DJ sessions a month, featuring talents such as the Kill the DJ collective.

⭐ SOCIAL CLUB *Club*

☎ 01 43 35 25 48; www.parissocialclub .com; 142 Rue Montmartre; entry free-€15; ⏱ 11pm-6am Wed-Sat; Ⓜ Grands Boulevards or Bourse

Here's another venue with all the latest sounds, specialising in electro. A collective of architects was commissioned to design its futuristic décor with neon lights.

⭐ REX CLUB *Club*
☎ 01 42 36 10 96; www.rexclub.com; 5 blvd Poissonnière; entry free-€15; 🕑 from 11pm or midnight Wed-Sat; Ⓜ Bonne Nouvelle

Many call this the best music venue in Paris. Its success has known no bounds since Laurent Garnier started the techno scene here. House, techno and electro can always be heard here.

⭐ FAVELA CHIC
Club, Restaurant
☎ 01 40 21 38 14; www.favelachic .com;18 Rue du Faubourg du Temple; free entry Tue-Thu, weekend tickets from €10; 🕑 8pm-2am Tue-Thu, to 4am Fri & Sat; Ⓜ République

Laid out like a cafeteria with long tables and benches plus a dance floor, this place knows how to party Brazilian style. Clients drink caipirinhas to frenzied samba rhythms and the motto 'chaos and progress' is followed to the letter by the droves of nightowls who flock here, often filling it to capacity.

⭐ NEW MORNING *Jazz*
☎ 01 45 23 51 41; www.newmorning .com; 7-9 Rue des Petites Écuries;

€15-25; 🕑 live music at 9pm; Ⓜ Château d'Eau

The superb acoustics in this old printing works make the New Morning a great place to listen to the jazz greats or other styles of music, featuring blues, rock, funk, salsa, Brazilian and Afro-Cuban sounds.

⭐ BIZZ'ART *Jazz & Soul Club*
☎ 01 40 34 70 00; www.bizzartclub .com; 167 Quai de Valmy; gigs €6-10, parties €10; 🕑 Wed-Sun; Ⓜ Louis Blanc

Same staff, same style, but with a new name – the Opus is now the Bizz'art. When the Canal was just taking off, this club was already drawing crowds with its soul, jazz and world sounds. Live music and DJs from 11pm, parties and dances on some Thursdays and Sundays (Brazilian Forro, tango, salsa…). Sit at the stylish bar or in a cosy corner next to the chimney. In the evening, a restaurant opens on the mezzanine level.

⭐ LE LIMONAIRE
Chansons
☎ 01 45 23 33 33; www.limonaire.free .fr; 18 Cité Bergère; free entry; 🕑 6pm-midnight Tue-Sat, from 7pm Sun; Ⓜ Grands Boulevards

This quintessentially Parisian wine bar puts on excellent live nights featuring French *chanson* (song) – a far cry from the bright lights of the larger venues in the district.

François Missonnier,
Founder and director of the Rock en Seine Festival

Rock en Seine and the Park de Saint-Cloud – an unlikely match, isn't it? And it took me a year and a half to find this gem of a place! The park, with its listed gardens, is set to welcome around 35,000 people for three days of music. This is a beautiful place, which fires your imagination and allows you to leave the city behind. We are also carrying on the tradition of putting on shows that was started with Marie-Antoinette! **What are your favourite nightspots?** I like starting the evening with a drink, watching a band. L'International, La Flèche d'Or (p113) and Le Scopitone are great meeting places, thanks to their regular line-up and friendly atmospheres. If I just want to listen to the music, I tend to go to Le Nouveau Casino (p114), La Maroquinerie (p114) and Le Point Éphémère (p61). Summer is the time for open-air concerts in parks with Paris Quartier d'Été. **What about food?** I live and work near the Canal Saint-Martin and the two places I enjoy eating at regularly, with fresh and original bistro-style cooking, are really close by, namely Le Villaret and Les P'tites Indécises.

L'International: 01 49 29 76 45; www.linternational.fr; 5-7 Rue Moret, 11th
Le Scopitone: 01 42 60 64 45; www.scopitoneclub.com; 5 Av. de l'Opéra, 1st
Le Villarets: 01 43 57 89 76; 13 Rue Ternaux, 11th
Les P'tites Indécises: 01 43 57 26 00; 2 Rue des Trois-Bornes, 11th

Rock en Seine (www.rockenseine.com) is *the* rock and pop festival in Paris. Three open-air stages are set up in the Domaine National de Saint-Cloud on the outskirts of Paris. A terrific programme line-up, combining cult bands and young talent. Runs the last weekend in August.

> THE LEFT BANK: CHIC GALLERIES AND EXCLUSIVE SHOPS

It's had some tough acts to follow, but the Left Bank has moved on from the time when Jean-Paul Sartre and Simone de Beauvoir called the shots in Saint-Germain des Prés. Nowadays, cultural life revolves less around literary figures (there aren't even that many bookshops here any more) and focuses more on secret, less well-established places, such as galleries hidden away in the courtyards of town houses. Likewise, while exploring the shopping streets around the Rue du Bac looking at the shops, it's easy to miss the Dina Vierny Foundation – Maillol Museum. The Galerie des Gobelins and the Henri Cartier-Bresson Foundation are also similarly tucked out of sight.

Art dealers, publishers and shoppers rub shoulders in the bistros and cafés, joined by students in between classes or having an evening drink. The neighbourhood has many *bistronomique* eateries (like gastropubs), which have been doing well in Paris recently. To the south, Issy-les-Moulineaux joined the technological revolution in its infancy, so it's not surprising to find Le Cube there, a venue dedicated to digital creativity.

THE LEFT BANK

◎ SEE
Cartier Foundation for
  Contemporary Art.....1 E6
Dina Vierny Foundation–
  Maillol Museum.........2 D2
Galerie des Gobelins 3 H6
Galerie Down Town...... 4 F2
Galerie Kamel Mennour5 F2
Galerie Kreo.................. 6 F2
Henri Cartier-Bresson
  Foundation 7 D6
Le Cube.........................8 A6
Magnum Gallery 9 E2

🛍 SHOP
Brand Bazar................10 D3
La Grande Epicerie
  du Bon Marché.........11 D3
Petite Mendigote 12 E2
Pierre Hermé 13 E2
Sentou........................14 D2
Vanessa Bruno...... 15 F3

🍴 EAT
Chez Gladines.............16 F6
Cosi.............................17 F2
L'Ami Jean..................18 A1
L'Avant-Goût 19 F6
Le Cinq Mars..............20 D1
Le Comptoir...............21 F3

Le Pré Verre................22 G3
Les Symples de
  l'Os à Moëlle 23 C5
Ze Kitchen Galerie......24 F2

🍷 DRINK
Bar du Marché 25 F2
La Palette 26 F2
L'Alcazar................... 27 F2
Mosquée de Paris...... 28 H5

⭐ PLAY
Le Wagg.................(See 27)

See map on following pages

◉ SEE

Although shops may have replaced many of the old bookstores, they haven't managed to engulf the area containing the galleries and other contemporary art, design and photography exhibition venues.

◉ CARTIER FOUNDATION FOR CONTEMPORARY ART

☎ 01 42 18 56 50, nomadic nights 01 42 18 56 72; www.fondation.cartier. com; 261 blvd Raspail; full price/concs €6.50/4.50; 🕒 11am-8pm Tue-Sun, to 10pm on Tue; Ⓜ Raspail; 🚻

This completely transparent venue, designed by Jean Nouvel, is a stunning setting for contemporary art. The five large exhibitions held every year are opportunities, for the Foundation, to observe and showcase new artists as much as to commission works. The carefully constructed individual-artist or themed exhibitions range from photography (including Robert Adams, Raymond Depardon and Herb Ritts), video, (including Agnès Varda and Patti Smith), painting (including David Lynch and Takeshi Kitano), sculpture (including César, JM Othoniel and Ron Mueck) and installations to design and fashion. The *soirées nomades* (nomadic nights) provide an insight into theatre and performance arts (music, dance, cinema) that are connected to the exhibitions.

The Cartier Foundation's leafy glass building

Don't forget to take a wander in the wonderful garden designed by Lothar Baumgarten.

◉ HENRI CARTIER-BRESSON FOUNDATION

☎ 01 56 80 27 00; www.henricartier bresson.org; 2 Impasse Lebouis; full price/concs €6/3; 🕒 1-6.30pm Tue-Fri & Sun, 11am-6.45pm Sat, to 8.30pm on Wed; Ⓜ Gaîté or Edgar Quinet

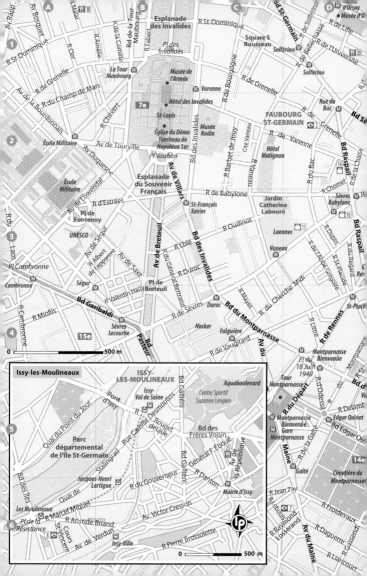

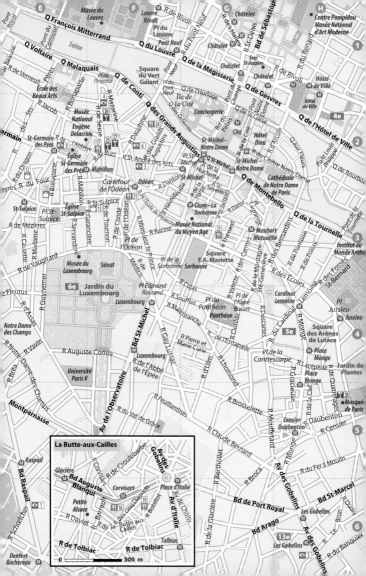

GALLERIES IN THE CARRÉ

Along with Le Marais, the Left Bank is an area of Paris with a high concentration of galleries, some of which are really worth a visit.

Galerie Kamel Mennour (☎ 01 56 24 03 63; www.kamelmennour.fr; 47 Rue Saint-André des Arts; ⏱ 11am-7pm Tue-Sat; Ⓜ Saint-Michel) Kamel Menour first made a name for himself by exhibiting ccontemporary photography before branching out into other media. Now his gallery has featured the work of artists such as Daniel Buren, Tadashi Kawamata, Claude Lévêque, Miri Segal and Martin Parr.

Galerie Kreo (☎ 01 53 10 23 00, www.galeriekreo.com; 31 Rue Dauphine; ⏱ 11am-7pm Tue-Sat; Ⓜ Odéon) This gallery, specialising in design (featuring work by Pierre Charpin, Martin Szekely, Alessandro Mendini and Christophe Pillet) has relocated from the 13th arrondissement to a 450-sq-metre duplex inside a historic building on the Left Bank.

Galerie Down Town (☎ 01 46 33 82 41; www.galeriedowntown.com; 33 Rue de Seine; ⏱ 10.30am-1pm and 2pm-7pm Tue-Sat; Ⓜ Mabillon) A fan of furniture by 1950s designers, François Laffanour sells pieces by Jean Prouvé, Charlotte Perriand, Pierre Jeanneret, Le Corbusier and George Nakashima.

Roughly 100 galleries have joined forces with antique dealers to form the **Carré Rive Gauche** association (www.carrerivegauche.com) in an area bordered by Rue des Saints-Pères, Rue de l'Université, Rue du Bac and the Quai Voltaire. The association organises regular events and you can use its website to search for items by type and speciality.

Housed in a former artists' workshop, the Henri Cartier-Bresson Foundation mainly exhibits work from its co-founder's photo agency, Magnum. Temporary exhibitions focus on other photographers, as well as painters, sculptors and designers. One such exhibition is dedicated to the winner of the HCB, a prize in aid of creativity awarded every two years, by an international jury, to a photographer whose work takes a documentary angle. Past winners include Fazal Sheikh and Jim Goldberg. The space on the 3rd floor under the glass roof is just gorgeous.

Ⓖ DINA VIERNY FOUNDATION – MAILLOL MUSEUM

☎ 01 42 22 59 58; www.museemaillol .com; 61 Rue de Grenelle; full price/concs €11/9; ⏱ 10.30am-7pm Wed-Mon, to 9.30pm Fri; Ⓜ Rue du Bac

Dina Vierny was not only a model and muse for Aristide Maillol, but also a collector and gallery owner. She collected major artwork from the 20th century – including works by Gauguin, Bonnard, Kandinsky and Henri Rousseau – as well as sculptures by Maillol and a collection of drawings, which are on display in the Hôtel Bouchardon. Temporary exhibitions regularly feature, such as the highly popular *C'est la Vie ! Vanités de Caravage à Damien Hirst* in 2010.

MAGNUM GALLERY
☎ 01 46 34 42 59; www.magnumgallery .fr; 13 Rue de l'Abbaye; free entry; 🕑 11am-7pm Tue-Sat; Ⓜ Saint-Germain des Prés

On the ground floor of the photography and art publisher Robert Delpire, and a stone's throw from the Place Saint-Germain des Prés, Magnum couldn't have imagined a better place for its new gallery which opened in the autumn of 2009. Four exhibitions are to be held there each year, with works selected from the archives of the prestigious agency – nearly 80 photographers, including Martin Parr, Lise Sarfati, Marc Riboud and Antoine d'Agata.

GALERIE DES GOBELINS
☎ 01 40 51 38 38; 42 Av des Gobelins; www.mobiliernational.culture.gouv .fr; full price/concs €6/4, guided tours €10/7.50; 🕑 11am-6pm Tue-Sun during temporary exhibitions; Ⓜ Gobelins

This gallery displays objects such as furniture, wall hangings and carpets from the collection of the Mobilier National, once the furnisher of royal palaces, now the provider of furnishings for the Palais de l'Élysée. Since 1964, it has been home to a research and design studio where furniture is studied and

Through the window of the Magnum Gallery

manufactured, based on projects commissioned to designers such as Pierre Paulin, Jean-Michel Wilmotte, Richard Peduzzi, and, more recently, Erwan and Ronan Bouroullec, Matali Crasset and Martin Szekely.

SHOP

The Left Bank has become a top shopping area, so the once intellectual Saint-Germain des Prés is now more of a fashion centre. The major fashion houses are all prominently positioned here and the neighbourhood is swarming with trendy boutiques, especially along the Rue du Cherche-Midi. The Left Bank also has great food shops.

LA GRANDE ÉPICERIE DU BON MARCHÉ
Specialist Food Shop
☎ 01 44 39 81 00; www.lagrande epicerie.fr; 38 Rue de Sèvres; 🕑 8.30am-9pm Mon-Sat; Ⓜ Sèvres Babylone

Le Cube, a centre for creative digital projects, in Issy-les-Moulineaux

London has the Harrods Food Hall, New York has Dean and Deluca, while Paris has La Grande Épicerie du Bon Marché. Here you can find obscure brands of mineral water, rare kinds of olive oil and a host of other gourmet treasures. Not just offering fabulous fresh produce, the stalls themselves are a feast for the eyes. This is a gourmet Paris must-see, even if you end up leaving with only a bag of pasta.

☐ PIERRE HERMÉ
Pâtisserie
☎ 01 43 54 47 77; www.pierreherme.com; 72 Rue Bonaparte; ☯ 10am-7pm Sun-Fri, to 7.30pm Sat; Ⓜ Saint-Sulpice
Just like a fashion designer, Pierre Hermé creates collections, with his world-famous macaroons taking pride of place as the final pièce de résistance. He first made a name for himself with his shop in Saint-Germain des Prés – sleek and unpretentious, much like his creations.

☐ VANESSA BRUNO *Fashion*
☎ 01 43 54 41 04; www.vanessabruno .com; 25 Rue Saint-Sulpice; ☯ 10.30am-7.20pm Mon-Sat; Ⓜ Mabillon or Odéon
The natural and feminine clothes sold here enchant Parisian women who love layers, silk, lace detailing and delicate materials. The boutique is lovely and bright, especially when you reach the 1st floor.

☐ BRAND BAZAR *Fashion*
☎ 01 45 44 40 02; www.brandbazar.fr; 33 Rue de Sèvres; ☯ 10.30am-7.30pm Mon-Sat; Ⓜ Sèvres Babylone
This large store is in cheerful contrast to other places in the Left Bank, which can sometimes seem a little straight-laced. T-shirts are piled up, clothes strewn haphazardly on

DIGITAL ISSY

The town of Issy-les-Moulineaux caught on to new technology very quickly, so it's no surprise to discover that **Le Cube** (☎ 01 58 88 30 00; www.lesiteducube.com; 20 Cours Saint-Vincent; exhibitions, events and conferences open to the public, videos/performances, concerts €3/5/7; 🕑 noon-7pm Tue-Sat, to 9pm Tue & Thu; **M** Mairie d'Issy then bus 123, stop Chemin des Vignes; or RER C Issy; or T2 Les Moulineaux) was built here. This space dedicated to creative digital works, flocked to by both artists (residents) and the public, puts on regular exhibitions, performances, projections, events and debates on all areas of digital art (mostly on Sundays and Thursdays). Every three years, Le Cube also organises a festival involving digital installations in the town.

For a great meal at a communal table with fellow diners, head to **Les Symples de l'Os à Moëlle** (☎ 01 41 08 02 52 ; www.lessymples.fr; 18 Av. de la République; 🕑 lunch & dinner Mon-Fri, dinner only Sat; **M** Mairie d'Issy), where a reasonably priced set menu (lunch/dinner €22/25) is on offer with large portions. There are some lovely traditional dishes and bookings are compulsory (the restaurant can only seat about 20 people inside).

hangers, shoes lined up on the floor, but behind what seems to be one big jumble sale lies a great selection of designer clothes (Manoush, See by Chloé, Antik Batik, Nolita, Anonymous) and an excellent choice of jeans.

🏠 PETITE MENDIGOTE
Accessories

☎ 01 42 84 20 07; www.petitemendigote
.fr; 23 Rue du Dragon; 🕑 1-7pm Mon,
11am-7pm Tue-Fri, 10.30am-7.30pm
Sat; **M** Saint-Germain des Prés or Sèvres
Babylone

This charming boutique is reminiscent of a boudoir – an altogether appropriate backdrop for the range of young, girly accessories it sells. Everyone is sure to be able to find a look to flatter them from

the different styles, materials, prints and colours on offer. The little clutch bags with slogans are very popular and items are reasonably priced.

🏠 SENTOU *Furniture, Design*

☎ 01 45 49 00 05; www.sentou.fr;
26 blvd Raspail; 🕑 2-7pm Mon, 10am-
7pm Tue-Sat; **M** Rue du Bac or Sèvres
Babylone

A stable of talented designers collaborates with Sentou to come up with the store's collection of furniture, lighting and home accessories, including reproductions of work by Isamu Noguchi. Tsé & Tsé, Ronan and Erwan Bouroullec and 100Drine are just a few of the savvy designers this boutique features, with its entire collection displayed over several floors.

Designer pieces and bold colours in Sentou (p71)

🍽 EAT

Many creative young chefs have flocked to this neighbourhood to offer reasonably priced, innovative and sometimes even semigastronomic dishes in décors that remain simple yet fashionable.

🍽 COSI
Italian, Sandwiches €

☎ 01 46 33 35 36; 54 Rue de Seine; ⊙ 11am-11pm; Ⓜ Mabillon

Get delicious hot bread fresh from the oven filled with your own choice of ingredients at Cosi, or you could go for a set combination such as the delicious Stonker (tomato, mozzarella, basil and rocket). The shop often plays opera in the café upstairs, where the walls are hung with paintings.

🍽 LE PRÉ VERRE
Gastropub €€

☎ 01 43 54 59 47; www.lepreverre.com; 8 Rue Thénard; ⊙ Tue-Sat; Ⓜ Maubert Mutualité

Wouldn't it be great if there were more places like this? The food is peppered with a playful blend of spices and can be delightfully surprising, the lunch menu is competitive and the atmosphere is chatty and laid-back as you would expect in a bistro where the menu and wine list are chalked up on slates on the walls.

🍽 LE CINQ MARS
Bistro €€-€€€

☎ 01 45 44 69 13; 54 Rue de Verneuil; ⊙ Mon-Sat; Ⓜ Rue du Bac or Solférino

This discreet bistro has a very Left Bank atmosphere. With a lovely wooden bar, high ceiling and tiled floor, its modern décor flits between minimalism and cosy touches. As far as the food is concerned, the menu trots out some excellent classic dishes (grilled steak with sea salt, fillet of cod with a caper sauce), while the wine list offers some exciting discoveries.

🍽 LE COMPTOIR
Gastropub €€€

☎ 01 43 29 12 05; 9 Carrefour de l'Odéon; ⊙ brasserie noon-6pm Mon-Fri, to 11pm Sat & Sun, gourmet restaurant from 8.30pm Mon-Fri; Ⓜ Odéon

HEAD FOR LA BUTTE-AUX-CAILLES

Less touristy than the hill in Montmartre, the Butte-aux-Cailles, which is 63m high, is a charming spot with a tumultuous past (evident in the names of cafés which refer to the famous song 'Le Temps des Cerises', composed for the Paris Commune). To get a feel for the neighbourhood, stroll down the Rue de la Butte-aux-Cailles by all means, but don't forget to explore the Rue des Cinq Diamants, Passage Barrault or Place Paul-Verlaine. Make a detour to number 10, Rue Daviel, where you'll find a spot called **Petite Alsace**, a cluster of social housing built in 1912, imitating the region's half-timbered buildings.

Stop to enjoy a meal at **Chez Gladines** (☎ 01 45 80 70 10; 30 Rue des Cinq-Diamants; Ⓜ Place d'Italie) *the* Parisian bistro, renowned for its Basque dishes, or head back towards the Place d'Italie, to **L'Avant-Goût** (☎ 01 53 80 24 00; 26 Rue Bobillot; ☽ Tue-Sat; Ⓜ Place d'Italie), to try Christophe Beaufront's famous contemporary dishes inspired by traditional recipes.

Yves Camdeborde, the inventor of the modern gastropub (otherwise known as the *bistronomique* kitchen), has now turned his talents to an art deco bistro on Carrefour de l'Odéon. A brasserie at lunch time, *bistronomique* dishes are on offer in the evening. Bookings are compulsory.

🍴 L'AMI JEAN
Gastropub €€€
☎ 01 47 05 86 89; 27 Rue Malar; ☽ Tue-Sat; Ⓜ La Tour Maubourg or RER C Pont de l'Alma

Don't let the rustic décor and the Bayonne hams hanging from the rafters fool you: this place is not your traditional Basque restaurant. It's a trendy spot where Stéphane Jégo's innovative food and generous portions draw diners towards this little gem tucked away in the 7th arrondissement.

🍴 ZE KITCHEN GALERIE
Fusion €€€
☎ 01 44 32 00 32; www.zekitchen galerie.fr; 4 Rue des Grands-Augustins; ☽ lunch & dinner Mon-Fri, dinner only Sat; Ⓜ Saint-Michel

You can see chef William Ledeuil at work in the open kitchen, creating mouth-watering dishes whose flavours intermingle, complemented by seasonings inspired by his travels and the tastes of Southeast Asia. Also inspired by contemporary art, the chef is not afraid to blend the Kitchen with a gallery.

🍸 DRINK

The classic venues Café de Flore, Les Deux Magots and Brasserie Lipp are still symbolic of the Left Bank's intellectual heritage but the spirit of Saint-Germain is also alive and well elsewhere, in less well-known places which draw a younger, livelier crowd.

▼ MOSQUÉE DE PARIS
Tea House

☎ 01 45 35 97 33; www.mosquee-de-paris.org; 2 bis Place du Puits de l'Ermite; ☼ tea room 9am-midnight; Ⓜ Censier Daubenton or Place Monge; ♿

This mosque is sure to take you away to exotic places, set in a 1920s mosque – a stunning example of Moorish Art Deco. As well as visiting the magnificent tea room, you can stroll through the cloistered courtyards to take a look at the ancient manuscripts in the library, unless you'd rather take a steam bath.

▼ BAR DU MARCHÉ *Bar*

☎ 01 43 26 55 15; 75 Rue de Seine; ☼ 8am-2pm; Ⓜ Mabillon

The waiters may be dressed as Paris street urchins, but the atmosphere here is far from retro. The terrace is full to bursting and you'll have to squeeze your way to the counter. Drinks flow freely, accompanied by popcorn or crisps. Tables are so packed that new friendships are easily struck up. Who is it that goes there? Bourgeois bohemians and dandies, of course!

▼ LA PALETTE *Café*

☎ 01 43 26 68 15; 43 Rue de Seine; ☼ 8am-2am; Ⓜ Mabillon

One of Henry Miller's favourite

places, this mirror-lined café has also welcomed the artists Cézanne and Braque. Nowadays, it draws gallery owners, students from the nearby architecture school and publishers, joined by a trendy crowd at night. Try the delicious Tartines Poilâne (toasties using renowned Poilâne bread) with a glass of wine. The café also has a nice terrace.

▼ L'ALCAZAR *Bar*

☎ 01 53 10 19 99; 62 Rue Mazarine; ☼ noon-3pm and 7pm-1am, to 2am Fri & Sat; Ⓜ Odéon

Alcazar's mezzanine bar, formerly a famous cabaret bar, is now a fashionable spot where you can get a bite to eat with your drink. The restaurant below, underneath the high glass roof, serves traditional French food. DJs play from Wednesday to Saturday.

⭐ PLAY

 LE WAGG *Club*

☎ 01 55 42 22 01; www.wagg.fr; 62 Rue Mazarine; €12; ☼ 11.30pm-dawn Fri & Sat, 3pm-midnight Sun; Ⓜ Odéon

Le Wagg is a friendly club where the music tends towards house, hip-hop or funk, with a Friday night Carwash and a Saturday night Groove Comittee or Golden Eighties. Sunday afternoon salsa classes are followed by Cuban-themed evenings.

>BERCY, LA GRANDE BIBLIOTHÈQUE AND IVRY: PARIS OF THE FUTURE

This flourishing neighbourhood was still undergoing huge changes just a few years ago. The Bibliothèque Nationale de France paved the way by relocating to the site of the former railway line. Indeed, the sheer scale of the redevelopment works underway in the area stretching from the Gare d'Austerlitz to the Boulevard Masséna, and bordered on either side by the River Seine and the Rue Chevaleret, is reminiscent of Haussmann's extensive modernisation of Paris in the 19th century. Each area has been entrusted to different urban planners, such as Christian de Portzamparc and the landscape architect Thierry Huau, who took on the challenge of the Masséna-Nord neighbourhood, near the new university campus. You can still see relics from the area's past resembling an industrial wasteland, such as the old railway cold-storage buildings (Les Frigos) converted into artists' studios.

Of course, the Seine adds to the neighbourhood's charm with music venues on board boats moored to the river banks and a new footbridge across to Bercy. The Crédac centre nearby in Ivry-sur-Seine and the MAC/VAL museum in Vitry have also done their part in spreading contemporary art around the city.

BERCY, LA GRANDE BIBLIOTHÈQUE AND IVRY

◉ SEE

This neighbourhood is full of interesting architecture: don't forget to look skywards or to explore the neighbouring streets, especially around the Université Paris 7-Diderot campus in the Masséna area.

◉ BIBLIOTHÈQUE NATIONALE DE FRANCE (BnF)

☎ 01 53 79 59 59; www.bnf.fr; 11 Quai François Mauriac; exhibitions full price/ concs €7/5; ⏲ exhibitions 10am-7pm Tue-Sat, 1-7pm Sun; Ⓜ Quai de la Gare or Bibliothèque François-Mitterrand (or RER C); ♿

The national library's four towers, designed by Dominique Perrault, are L-shaped, like open books. 79m high, they house more than 10 million books, which are protected from the light by adjustable wooden shutters. Below the towers, the library is surrounded by a garden measuring more than one hectare. You can go on a tour from Tuesday to Friday at 2pm and at 3pm on Saturdays and Sundays (bookings ☎ 01 53 79 49 49). The BnF also has an interesting series of temporary exhibitions touching on a wide range of disciplines including photography, etching and contemporary art. Closed for several weeks in September.

◉ PARC DE BERCY

128 Quai de Bercy; ⏲ 8am-5.45pm, to 9.30pm in summer, from 9am weekends

The grounds of the BnF

& public holidays; Ⓜ Bercy or Cour Saint-Émilion

This modern park stands where former wine warehouses used to be, a past revealed by the old railway tracks and the 400 vines harvested every year. Located next to the Palais Omnisports de Paris Bercy (POPB) stadium, it is the perfect place to lie on the grass and relax or kick a ball around. You could also explore the garden dedicated to Yitzhak Rabin, with its nine sections (a vegetable garden, an orchard, a rose garden, a scented garden…). Overlooking the Rue Joseph Kessel, the Maison du Lac is surrounded by a romantic garden which makes a beautiful picnic spot. Get to the Simone de Beauvoir footbridge by walking up the central steps where a fountain splashes refreshing water in summer.

◎ CINÉMATHÈQUE FRANÇAISE

☎ 01 71 19 33 33; www.cinematheque.com; 51 Rue de Bercy; screenings full price/concs €6.50/5, museum €5/4, exhibitions €7/6, architectural tour €8/7 1st Sun of the month; ⏱ exhibitions noon-7pm Mon-Sat, to 10pm Thu, 10am-8pm Sun, closed Tue; Ⓜ Bercy; ♿
The building designed by the American architect Frank Gehry has been home to the Cinémathèque for several years now. As well as numerous screenings, temporary exhibitions and other major festivals (*Jacques Tati, deux temps, trois mouvements* or *Dennis Hopper et le nouvel Hollywood*), the Musée du Cinéma features the Cinémathèque's collections since it was established in 1936, illustrated with the aid of exhibits such as films, cameras, posters and costumes.

◎ BÉTONSALON

☎ 01 45 84 17 56; www.betonsalon.net; 9 Esplanade Vidal-Naquet; free entry; ⏱ noon-9pm Wed-Sat, closed in August; Ⓜ Boulevard Masséna or RER C Bibliothèque François Mitterrand; ♿
Located at the heart of the Université Paris 7, in the Halle aux Farines, Bétonsalon nurtures young talents who dare to be different.

Dedicated to many disciplines, this art and research centre allows artists, students, philosophers, choreographers, scientists and so on to interact. Exhibitions, public events and performance cycles, including some open-air evening screenings, are organised throughout the year.

◎ SIMONE DE BEAUVOIR FOOTBRIDGE

Ⓜ Quai de la Gare or Bercy; ♿
This charming footbridge links the Parc de Bercy and the Bibliothèque nationale de France, allowing you to cross the river on foot. Designed by Austrian architect Dietmar Feichtinger, the footbridge soars gracefully across the Seine with no supports touching the water, giving

Graceful lines of the Simone de Beauvoir footbridge

HOT TALENT IN LES FRIGOS

It's hard to miss the former SNCF (national railway company) cold-storage buildings (Les Frigos) which were decommissioned when the food market moved to Rungis. The SNCF put part of this area up for rent in the 1980s. Attracted by this industrial wasteland, artists flocked here, gradually creating a whole city of artists, called, strangely enough, **Les Frigos** (http://les-frigos.com). Even today, it still looks like a squat underneath its layers of graffiti. Once under threat, and now surrounded by new buildings which have recently sprung up, Les Frigos have managed to retain their artistic values. The site opens it doors to the public every year in May. You can find the schedule for exhibitions and previews on the website above.

it a sleek profile. The arc above and the convex suspended bridge below form a central lens-shaped area between them, 106m in length. The space in the middle of the bridge is sometimes used for events (such as music events, second-hand book fairs and exhibitions).

◉ DOCKS EN SEINE
**28-36 Quai d'Austerlitz, btwn Charles de Gaulle & Bercy Bridges; Ⓜ Quai de la Gare, Gare d'Austerlitz
or Gare de Lyon; or Voguéo boat shuttle terminal**
This is one of Paris' latest great architectural achievements. Created to house the Institut Français de la Mode (IFM), together with shops, restaurants and cafés, and named the Cité de la Mode et du Design. These docks were built on the site of former warehouses dating back to 1907, whose concrete structures are still partly visible today. The architects Dominique Jakob and Brendan

MacFarlane have created an green structure in steel and glass which juts out from the face of the building, overlooking the Seine. Yann Kersalé provided the plants and lighting for the 2000-sq-metre roof terrace garden – a great place to relax.

◉ CRÉDAC
☎ 01 49 60 25 06; www.credac.fr; 93 Av Georges-Gosnat, Ivry-sur-Seine; free entry; ⏲ 2-6pm Tue-Fri, to 7pm Sat & Sun; Ⓜ Mairie d'Ivry or RER C Ivry-sur-Seine
Leaving no area unexplored and striving to engage the public, this contemporary art venue is a wonderful and daring experiment (recently featuring Pierre Vadi, Didier Rittener and Vincent Beaurin).

◉ JOSEPHINE BAKER SWIMMING POOL
☎ 01 56 61 96 50; www.piscines.paris .fr; Quai François Mauriac; Ⓜ Quai de la Gare

Malachi Farrell,
Contemporary Artist

You were born in Ireland, live in the suburbs in Malakoff and you're exhibiting in Paris. What kind of relationship do you have with the city? What's surprising is that I thought contemporary art was easier to design and exhibit in New York, but in fact I've realised that Paris is just as good a showcase for my work. All my exhibitions are about the urban environment, with its strengths and fragility. For the Dreamlands exhibition at the Pompidou Centre (p29), I also made use of the location, with the cardboard cut-out of New York being superimposed over the Parisien roofs visible from the windows. **Your name often crops up in connection to kinetic art…** I am often inspired by fairground attractions. My installations are triggered by the movements of people nearby. What motivates me is reaching out to the public, preferably to people who don't dare go into galleries, making them react or think about the current world. **Are there any specific places for projects like these?** I am also working on other projects, one at Mains d'Œuvres in Saint-Ouen (p129) and the other in Montreuil. But let's also give a mention to the MAC/VAL (opposite), my favourite museum in Paris, or on the outskirts to be more precise. In the end, it's the outskirts of the city that I like best! **What about a good place to eat?** Le Snack in Saint-Ouen, where you can eat bagels just like in New York.

Le Snack: 09 54 78 21 74 ; 8 Rue Claude-Monet, Saint-Ouen, Ⓜ Mairie de Saint-Ouen

NEIGHBOURHOODS

BERCY, LA GRANDE BIBLIOTHÈQUE AND IVRY

THE MAC/VAL

An enormous statue of Dubuffet at the Place de la Libération in Vitry marks the site of the first contemporary art museum to be built outside the centre of Paris. The **MAC/VAL** (☎ 01 43 91 64 20; www.macval.fr; Place de la Libération, Vitry-sur-Seine; full price/concs €5/2.50; ⏱ noon-7pm Tue-Sun; free entry 1st Sun of each month; Ⓜ T3 Porte de Choisy, then bus 183, stop Musée MAC/VAL). The Musée d'Art Contemporain du Val-de-Marne has become well established in the local area and is currently trying to reach a wider audience.

Designed by the architect Jacques Ripault, the building's sleek lines are pleasing to the eye. Built as a venue to house the museum's collections, this is a beautiful airy space in which to see the permanent exhibition, boosted by the regional contemporary art collection (Niki de Saint Phalle, Claude Closky, Ange Leccia, Jacques Monory, Christian Boltanski, Claude Levêque), featuring work from the French art scene of the 1950s to the present day (see the interview with Malachi Farrell, some of whose works have been acquired by the MAC/VAL, opposite). Themed exhibitions which change regularly provide a good overview of the museum's permanent collection. Temporary exhibitions are also organised. There is a bookshop on contemporary art and architecture, a huge garden and a restaurant, Le Chantier, to visit.

Paris hasn't had a swimming pool on the Seine since the Deligny baths were closed down in 1993. Moored at the foot of the national library, the floating swimming pool with a sliding sunroof and sun deck is very popular in summer. It is now once again possible to swim lengths while looking out onto the Seine.

🛍 SHOP

As yet uninspiring, shopping is bound to pick up in the area at some stage. That said, there is already a place to check out here: Bercy Village, home to fashion and design shops. Film buffs should head to the MK2-Bibliothèque shop for its fabulous selection of DVDs.

🛍 BERCY VILLAGE

☎ 0825 16 60 75; www.bercyvillage.com; 28 Rue François Truffaut; ⏱ shops 11am-9pm, restaurants to 2am; Ⓜ Cour Saint-Émilion

This long, cobbled pedestrian street is lined with old restored wine warehouses and rows of restaurants and shops, one after the other. Designer Agnès b has a boutique here showing her entire range. You will also find Nature et Découvertes and Résonances – both perfect for gift-buying inspiration along the lines of nature, health and beauty. There is a Fnac Éveil & Jeux for children's toys, Alice Délice for tableware and Boardriders, a shop dedicated to wintersports and watersports.

CODE NAME LOUISE 13

Over the past 10 years, the Rue Louise Weiss has made quite an impact on Paris' contemporary art scene with its endless row of galleries attracted here by the up-and-coming neighbourhood and its low rental prices. Many of these galleries have since moved on to the Marais, to the Left Bank (Galerie Kreo p68) or to Belleville (Galerie Suzanne Tarasiève; p108), but the street still remains a haven for art, although it is impossible to say how much longer this will last. Most of the neighbourhood's galleries belong to the **Louise 13** association (www.louise13.fr). This website provides preview dates (the same for all galleries), information on current exhibitions and the addresses of the galleries, which are generally closed on Sundays and Mondays.

⚒ EAT

You'll find large brasseries around the library and the Parc de Bercy or you can grab a quick bite to eat in the Café de l'Est inside the BnF (closed on Mondays). The MK2-Bibliothèque cinema also has a chic brasserie with comfy seats.

⚒ LE 51 *Picnic, Grill* €
☎ 01 58 51 10 91; 51 Rue de Bercy;
🕑 10am-5pm Mon, to11pm Wed-Sun;
Ⓜ **Bercy**

A wooden table which winds from the inside to the outside is doubtless one of the more telling details of this restaurant in the Cinémathèque (p78). Le 51 invites its customers to go outside, to picnic and dance in the Parc de Bercy – dances in the summer and Salsa Sundays in winter (free entry, 3pm to 8pm) and to come and sit down in the warm for a drink. The menu features salads, pâté and sandwiches, but also

roasted meat (whole chickens for groups!) and outdoor grills when the weather is good.

★ PLAY

In summer, the banks of the Seine by the Quai de la Gare turn into an attractive open-air music venue, drawing crowds to tables set up on the decks of moored boats. Live music is on offer all year round on board the boats.

★ BATOFAR *Live Music Venue, Club*
☎ 01 53 14 76 59; www.batofar.org;
opposite 11 Quai François Mauriac; entry
free-€15; 🕑 club Tue-Sat from 11pm;
Ⓜ **Quai de la Gare or Bibliothèque
François Mitterrand (or RER C)**

You can't fail to spot the Batofar, the unusual red riverboat housing four bars and a club in its hull. The 'flagship' venue for electro music, it also branches out towards other

Terraces, bars, concerts and club: there's something for everyone at the Batofar

genres (such as hip-hop, house and world music). In summer, the bridge deck opens from 6pm (4pm on Sundays) for deckchair drinks followed by concerts starting at midnight in its restaurant. There is a quayside restaurant in summer.

⭐ LA DAME DE CANTON
LIVE *Music Venue, Club*
☎ 01 53 61 08 49; www.damedecanton .com; opposite 11 Quai François Mauriac; concerts full price/concs €8-10/6-8, club €5; ⏱ 7pm-2am Tue-Thu, to dawn weekends Ⓜ Quai de la Gare or Bibliothèque François Mitterrand
Climb aboard this three-masted Chinese junk at the foot of the BnF for weekend DJ nights or party-like concerts (ranging from gypsy music

jazz-style to French song music with a twist or salsa). In summer, the 'beach bar' is open on the quayside. The restaurant is open all year round (dinner Tuesdays to Saturdays).

⭐ LE DJOON
Club
☎ 01 45 70 83 49; www.djoon.fr; 22 Bd Vincent-Auriol; €5-18; ⏱ from 11pm Fri & Sat, from 6pm Sun; Ⓜ Quai de la Gare
Large but less central, Le Djoon has a fine reputation thanks to its bill of soul, funk, house and garage. On Sundays, boogie fever takes over at Dance Culture nights; Thursdays lure an after-work crowd. Like the music, the décor is a transatlantic mix of modern and classic retro.

>BASTILLE, NATION AND MONTREUIL: A CULTURAL REVOLUTION

The decision to build a modern opera house for everyone to enjoy in the Bastille area was an attempt to rejuvenate the eastern side of Paris. Mission accomplished! Bastille was one of the first neighbourhoods to be described as 'trendy', with its lively areas such as Rue de Charonne and Rue de la Roquette.

There is no shortage of places to go out, have a drink, eat dinner, listen to music and dance. Try Les Disquaires for dancing and Unico for dining. However, this ever-changing cultural revolution hasn't destroyed the everyday life of this down-to-earth residential area. Take the fiercely loyal customers who frequent the Market d'Aligre for example, or the otherworldly Rue Paul Bert, which has succeeded in preserving its village feel. Adding to the local flavour is the Promenade Plantée, an open, partly elevated garden walkway, which weaves its way gently to the city gates.

Eastern expansion is still in full effect. Montreuil, a real hotbed of artists, is experiencing an influx of new talent in search of a more cosmopolitan culture, as well as being attracted to the area's friendly atmosphere.

BASTILLE, NATION AND MONTREUIL

See map on following pages

The steps of the Opéra Bastille are a popular meeting place for Parisians

👁 SEE

This neighbourhood is bursting with architectural and artistic achievements, from the Opéra Bastille, which has become a prominent public landmark, the Maison Rouge, an unusual venue housing contemporary art, to the more private galleries.

👁 OPÉRA BASTILLE

☎ 0892 89 90 90, guided tours 01 40 01 19 70; www.operadeparis.fr; Place de la Bastille, ticket booth 130 Rue de Lyon; guided tours full price/concs €11/9; 🕑 ticket office 10.30am-6.30pm Mon-Sat; Ⓜ Bastille; ♿

The building's façade is finally undergoing a facelift. Although the outside of the building designed by architect Carlos Ott aged more quickly than expected, the interior has stood up to the challenges of the huge productions staged there. Visit the public foyers (look out for the Niki de Saint-Phalle and Jean Tinguely sculptures), the performance hall and the backstage area when taking a tour of the opera house. If you fancy catching a performance, bear in mind that 62 standing places are available each night at the modest price of €5 at the door. You can also pick up special-rate tickets if there are spare seats left 15 minutes before the performance starts.

AN ORIGINAL GARDEN WALKWAY

A tree-lined, flowery 'green walkway', or **Promenade Plantée** (www.promenade-plantee .org) as it is known, runs the whole 4.5km length of the 12th arrondissement, following the course of the old railway line. It starts behind the Opéra Bastille, overlooking the Avenue Dausmenil, and ends at the Porte Dorée.

This unusual garden walkway with its flowerbeds, benches and raised pathway has been copied for similar projects in the UK and the US. The garden walkway is supported by the **Viaduc des Arts** (www.viaducdesarts.fr), home to craft shops which restore antiques and produce new items using traditional methods. Upholsterers, interior designers, furniture makers, string and woodwind instrument makers, needle workers and jewellers are just some of the craftsmen to be found here.

Bicycles are allowed on the walkway from the Allée Vivaldi, after the Jardin de Reuilly. Why not hire a bicycle using Vélib' (hire point at 42 Allée Vivaldi, see p159)? Then you can cycle all the way to the Porte Dorée and even to the Bois de Vincennes if the mood takes you!

🎦 PAVILLON DE L'ARSENAL

☎ 01 42 76 33 97; www.pavillon-arsenal.com; 21 Bd Morland; free entry; 🕓 10.30am-6.30pm Tue-Sat, 11am-7pm Sun; Ⓜ Sully Morland or Bastille; ♿

This typical 19th-century building, a former powder factory with a large, glass-roofed hall, houses an interesting permanent exhibition on architectural developments in Paris from past to present. One section is devoted to projects in progress and includes a large, up-to-date scale-model of Paris. There are also three temporary exhibitions on the 1st floor whose original presentation is usually worth the trip: come and ponder the future of Paris.

🎦 CITÉ NATIONALE DE L'HISTOIRE DE L'IMMIGRATION

☎ 01 53 59 58 60; www.histoire-immigration.fr; 293 Av Daumesnil; full price/concs entry during exhibition period €5/3.50, outside exhibition period €3/2; 🕓 10am-5.30pm Tue-Fri, to 7pm Sat & Sun; Ⓜ Porte Dorée; ♿

The first museum dedicated to the history of immigration, this centre can be found in the Palais de la Porte Dorée, a remarkable, art deco style building constructed for the Paris Colonial Exhibition in 1931. The permanent exhibition called *Repères* (landmarks) is a clever blend of individual stories and history relating to the mass waves of immigration to France, illustrated by photos, sound recordings and archive documents. There are also

The Viaduc des Arts: a walk of highs and lows

café-restaurant, guided tours at 4pm on Saturdays and Sundays and a schedule of cultural events in La Suite, designed to resemble a hotel room). Large international collections are exhibited, alternating with single-artist and themed projects. Experiences here are multifaceted and often outstanding, such as the *Vraoum! Trésors de la Bande Déssinée et Art Contemporain* and *Warhol TV* exhibitions. The Patio – a glass-covered area visible from the café – is a space regularly occupied by artists' installations, while a small vestibule displays the work of young artists whose work the gallery does not yet exhibit.

exhibitions exploring themes such as identity, borders, territory and other topics linked to the concept of multiculturalism.

🅖 LA MAISON ROUGE

☎ 01 40 01 08 81; www.lamaisonrouge .org; 10 blvd de la Bastille; full price/ concs €7/5, free entry for under-13s; 🕙 11am-7pm Wed-Sun, to 9pm Thu; Ⓜ Quai de la Rapée; 🕭

The Maison Rouge, set up by Antoine de Galbert as part of a private initiative, is an attractive exhibition space for contemporary work (the building is inside an old factory) and provides a warm, sociable setting (bookshop,

🅖 GALERIE VIA

☎ 01 46 28 11 11; www.via.fr; 29-35 Av Daumesnil; free entry; 🕙 10am-1pm and 2-6pm Mon-Fri, 1-6pm Sat & Sun; Ⓜ Gare de Lyon or Ledru-Rollin

VIA, short for Valorisation de l'Innovation dans l'Ameublement (Promoting Innovation in Interior Design), is an association which supports contemporary design (furniture, lighting, tableware, carpets, upholstery) by providing funding for prototypes, among other things. Six or seven exhibitions a year are put on in this space nestled under the Viaduc des Arts, and feature various creations with the VIA label given to items produced in partnership between a French manufacturer and a designer.

⊙ GALERIE PATRICK SEGUIN
☎ 01 47 00 32 35; www.patrickseguin
.com; 5 Rue des Taillandiers; free entry;
⏰ 10am-7pm Tue-Sat; Ⓜ Bastille or
Ledru-Rollin

This gallery, which specialises in
1950s furniture by designers such as
Jean Prouvé, Le Corbusier, Charlotte
Perriand, Jean Royère, Serge Mouille
and Alexandre Noll, is housed in
a former power plant renovated
by Jean Nouvel. It favours original
pieces over reproductions.

⊙ LE LIEU DU DESIGN
☎ 01 40 41 51 02; www.lelieududesign
.com; 74 Rue du Faubourg Saint-Antoine;
free entry; ⏰ 11am-6pm Tue-Sat;
Ⓜ Ledru-Rollin

This place, which promotes
industrial and ecodesign, has been
set up in a lovely passageway that
reminds visitors of the arts and
crafts tradition of the quartier. Apart
from a document centre (open 2pm
to 6pm Monday to Friday) and a
materials library (by appointment),
there is an exhibition area that
features several exhibitions a year,
reflecting the challenges (and
richness) of contemporary design,
such as the furniture prototypes
from the Dito collective in *Dito
from Scratch* in 2010 that reveal
an unexpected approach as their
designers have to meet constraints
regarding shapes, colour and
materials.

The Dito collective exhibition at the Lieu du Design

🛍 SHOP

In Bastille, head to the Rue Keller
for designer boutiques and manga
stores, or the Rue de Charonne,
another of the area's fashionable
haunts. Slightly off the beaten
track, the Rue Saint-Nicolas is home
to Louison, a delightful bag shop
and two Caravane interior design
boutiques, one dedicated to home
décor (number 19), the other selling
decorative craft items.

🛍 ISABEL MARANT *Fashion*
☎ 01 49 29 71 55; www.isabelmarant.tm
.fr; 16 Rue de Charonne; ⏰ 10.30am-
7.30pm Mon-Sat; Ⓜ Ledru-Rollin

Come and see why this designer's
urban bohemian pieces which
borrow shamelessly from more
masculine styles, have captivated

young, chic Parisian women all over the city. Étoile, Marant's secondary line, is more affordable than the main collection.

🏠 FRENCH TROTTERS *Fashion*
☎ 01 47 00 84 35; www.frenchtrotters
.fr; 30 Rue de Charonne; 🕑 2.30-7.30pm Mon, 11am-7.30pm Tue-Sat; Ⓜ Bastille or Ledru-Rollin

French Trotters unites designers from Paris, Scandinavia, New York, Japan and Australia, and provides a showcase for their accessories, menswear and women's clothing. Some of these designers are already well-established (Erotokritos, Gaspard Yurkievich, Émilie Casiez), while others are less well-known (Won Hundred, Something Else, Cynthia Vincent). Shows and/or events featuring the designers are often organised on the 1st floor.

🏠 GAËLLE BARRÉ *Fashion*
☎ 01 43 14 63 02; www.gaellebarre.com; 17 Rue Keller; 🕑 10.30am-8.30pm Tue-Sat; Ⓜ Bastille or Ledru-Rollin

What does Gaëlle Barré have to offer? Slightly retro cuts, feminine style and colourful prints. This is a great store for dresses and accessories as well as kids' clothing.

🏠 EN VILLE *Vintage Fashion*
☎ 01 43 71 07 30; www.enville-vintage
.fr; 13 Rue Paul Bert; 🕑 12.30-7.30pm Thur-Sat; Ⓜ Faidherbe Chaligny

Alexandra and David take part in the Puces du Design (Design Flea Markets) and the Vintage Salon, and work closely with stylists and costume designers as well as opening their vintage studio to the public. Here you'll find a wide range of clothes from the 1960s, 1970s and 1980s, featuring pieces from Courrèges, Cardin and Emilio Pucci, not to mention clothing and accessories (sunglasses and shoes) for both men and women.

🍴 EAT
Less famous than the restaurants in Bastille or Nation, Montreuil nevertheless has some good, lively little places to eat.

🍴 LA MUSE VIN *Wine Bar* €€
☎ 01 40 09 93 05; 101 Rue de Charonne; 🕑 wine bar 7pm-12.30am Mon-Sat, lunch Mon-Fri; Ⓜ Charonne

The wines on offer here are more exciting than the food, which tends towards the traditional with dishes such as strips of veal Milanaise or stuffed squid. The bright setting creates a modern feel and the display of bottles is delightful.

🍴 LA GROSSE MIGNONNE
Bistro €€
☎ 01 42 87 54 51; www.lagrosse
mignonne.com; 56 Rue Carnot, Montreuil; 🕑 dinner Mon-Sun, lunch Tue-Sat; Ⓜ Croix de Chavaux

A charming, child-friendly bistro with a corner full of toys and

A TASTE OF PARIS AT THE ALIGRE MARKET

Many Parisians would do anything to have a market like this nearby. The **Aligre Market** (Marché d'Aligre) is open every day except Mondays from 8.30am to 1pm between the Rue d'Aligre and Place d'Aligre, and is an incredibly lively little world of its own. It sells high-quality products at reasonable prices. The indoor Marché Beauveau with its specialist stalls and the flea market complete the set. Once you've filled your basket, head to the **Baron Rouge** (☎ 01 43 43 14 32; ☷ 10am-3pm and 5-10pm Tue-Thu, 10am-10pm Fri & Sat, 10am-4pm Sun; 1 Rue Théophile-Roussel), for a pre-lunch glass of wine and sit in the bar at the back or at one of the tables outside, stacked up on wine crates!

teddies as well as a little library area between the bar and the restaurant. The décor is a mix of old-fashioned chairs and simple modern dining tables. On the menu are huge steaks, kangaroo with a tarragon cream sauce or more classic dishes in the vein of grilled prawns or rack of lamb. This venue often hosts concerts and exhibitions.

🍴 LA CAVE EST RESTAURANT
Wine Bar   €€

☎ 01 42 87 09 48; www.lacaveest restaurant.com; 45 Rue de Paris, Montreuil; ☷ Mon-Sat; Ⓜ Croix de Chavaux

The entrance first leads to a wine cellar (wine-tasting one Wednesday a month at 8pm) with a carpeted wooden floor and a little delicatessen. Further back there is a restaurant which enjoys an excellent reputation. The menu is well thought-out and offers some delicious dishes.

BISTROT PAUL BERT
Bistro €€€

☎ 01 43 72 24 01; 18 Rue Paul Bert; Tue-Sat; M Faidherbe Chaligny

You can have your steak cooked anyway you like here: rare, blue or undercooked. This should give you an idea of this typical Parisian bistro which sticks shamelessly to its guns regardless of the ever-changing food fashions. In fact, this is precisely what has the bourgeois bohemian arty crowd lining up at its door.

UNICO *Argentine* €€€

☎ 01 43 67 68 08; www.resto-unico .com; 15 Rue Paul Bert; Tue-Sat, dinner only Mon; M Faidherbe Chaligny

This new Latin American restaurant transports you to the 1970s with its orange and brown décor. The restaurant has retained some of the features of the old butcher's shop it took over. The meat – chargrilled in the traditional manner – comes straight from Argentina. The bread and vegetables are the only local items on the menu!

DRINK

Bastille offers plenty of places to have a drink other than the Rue de

Lappe, which attracts large crowds due to its many bars and restaurants.

PAUSE CAFÉ *Café*

☎ 01 48 06 80 33; 41 Rue de Charonne; Mon-Sat, lunch only Sun; M Ledru-Rollin

Pause Café has been the favourite haunt of the neighbourhood's fashionable set ever since it opened. The stylish 1950s mosaic floor and the large terrace (which is heated in winter) are admittedly the venue's most attractive features.

BOTTLE SHOP *Pub*

☎ 01 43 14 28 04; 5 Rue Trousseau; noon-2am; M Ledru-Rollin

A good place to get a drink and enjoy the friendly atmosphere reminiscent of an English pub (more due to the dominant nationality of customers than the décor). Don't miss out on happy hour or the DJs who play rock music on the weekend.

BISTROT DU MARCHÉ
Bar

☎ 01 42 87 05 12; 9 Place du Marché; 7.30-midnight; M Croix de Chavaux

This place is the life and soul of Montreuil. The bar's décor is plain and simple, with school chairs providing perfectly good seating. The sparkling atmosphere is down to the clientele, a combination of artists and bourgeois bohemians. Concerts are regularly held, especially on Sundays.

NEIGHBOURHOODS

BASTILLE, NATION AND MONTREUIL

Inside the sophisticated Pause Café (p93)

★ PLAY

There are concerts to suit almost every musical taste in this vibrant and cosmopolitan part of eastern Paris.

★ POP IN Music Venue

☎ 01 48 05 56 11; www.popin.fr; 105 Rue Amelot; free entry; ⏰ 6.30pm-1.30am, to 2am Thu-Sat; Ⓜ Saint-Sébastien Froissart

This place is a must if you love Britpop or indie rock music. Give it a miss if you don't like confined spaces though – gigs take place in the cellar! Another great option in the area is a farily similar venue on the same street: the Zéro Zéro at 89 Rue Amelot.

★ PANIC ROOM Bar, Club

☎ 01 58 30 93 43; www.myspace.com/gotopanicroom; 101 Rue Amelot; free entry; ⏰ 6pm-2am Tue-Sat; Ⓜ Saint-Sébastien Froissart

Somewhere between the Zéro Zéro and the Pop In, this new nightclub has made its mark featuring rock-electro-pop – a real 'survival room' to counteract the stress of city living! Featuring an unusual cocktail menu, a cellar dancefloor, DJ sets and a basement smoking room.

★ SATELLIT CAFÉ World Music

☎ 01 47 00 48 87; www.satellit-cafe.com; 44 Rue de la Folie Méricourt; concerts full price/concs €10/8, club €10, free for women; ⏰ concerts Wed-Sat and some Tue 9pm, club 10pm to dawn Thu-Sat; Ⓜ Saint-Ambroise or Oberkampf

This music café gives all kinds of world music a go. During the week, from Monday to Thursday, there are concerts featuring young musicians as well as more famous artists. On the weekend, world music nights take over, so come and dance until daybreak to exotic rhythms from around the globe.

DISCOVER MONTREUIL

Montreuil is one of those suburban areas which attract Parisians by offering lower property prices compared to the city centre itself. Its industrial buildings are also perfect for loft or studio conversions. Although the town was famous until the end of the 19th century for producing peaches grown on trees trained against the walls, it became industrialised in the 20th century. The Festival des Murs-à-Pêche (Peach Wall Festival) in June every year celebrates this fact, while the names of cafés, restaurants and music venues such as the Grosse Mignonne (p91), named after a type of peach, and Café de la Pêche also commemorate this aspect of local history. Traces of this period remain visible in old factories such as the Établissements Chapal, where rabbit fur used to be tanned.

Another attraction is the **Puces de Montreuil** (Ⓜ Porte de Montreuil), a large flea market open every weekend from 7am to 7.30pm, which mostly features second-hand clothes, accessories and all sorts of other items.

The **Montreuil Tourist Office** (☎ 01 41 58 14 09; www.destinationmontreuil.fr; 1 Rue Kléber; 🕑 2-5.30pm Mon-Thu, 1-5.30pm Fri, 10am-noon Sat Oct-May, extended opening hours Thu-Fri Jun-Jul) offers walking tours of the area. There is also a pedestrian route between the town's three parks which takes around three and a half hours to walk when following the markings on the ground.

⭐ INSTANTS CHAVIRÉS
Experimental Music

☎ 01 42 87 25 91; www.instantschavires
.com; 7 Rue Richard Lenoir, Montreuil; full
price/concs €8/12; 🕑 doors open 8.30pm,
concerts from 9pm; Ⓜ Robespierre

Come to Instants Chavirés with a mind open to all kinds of musical experiments: expect improvisation and witness the birth of new music trends, which the former jazz venue is now famous for. A melting pot for electro-acoustic and established genres, noise and improvised music, this is a spot that also showcases the work of budding directors by showing a film before the start of every concert.

⭐ LE RESERVOIR
Live Music Venue, Club

☎ 01 43 56 39 60; www.reservoirclub
.com; 16 Rue de la Forge Royale; entry
free-€20; 🕑 restaurant/bar from 8pm
Tue-Sat, from 11.30am Sun; Ⓜ Ledru-
Rollin or Bastille

Mary de Vivo has adapted the Anglo-Saxon concept of an all-in-one club in the *quartier* of La Bastille, with a bar, restaurant, concerts (jazz, soul, pop, rock or French *chansons*), shows (cabaret evenings) and dancefloor after midnight. There's even musical brunch on Sundays (up to 4.30pm). It's worth going just for the décor, with tables and rococo chairs in front of the stage, frescoes, mirrors and coloured lamps.

>LE MARAIS: FASHION AND DESIGN AMID A THRIVING GAY SCENE

Le Marais has more going for it than its central Parisian location. It is also a hub of all things cool, setting and following design and fashion trends. Whether it's down to the co-existence of the gay and Jewish communities, the incredible number of art galleries or the cascading boutiques, this historic district is constantly reinventing itself. The Upper Marais (*le haut Marais*), which begins behind the Musée Picasso, is undergoing the sort of transformation only Paris can inspire. The buildings undergoing renovation are legion and designers are investing in property, often opening beautiful, innovative spaces. So far, the balance between old and new has been maintained. The district is still studded with places that are simultaneously of-the-moment and timeless. This is embodied by Open Café, a famous gay bar on the corner of Rue des Archives and Rue Sainte-Croix de la Bretonnerie, the Rue du Trésor (for its terraces sheltered from the traffic) and the Rue des Francs Bourgeois (for the Sunday window shopping), not to mention the chic Place des Vosges.

LE MARAIS

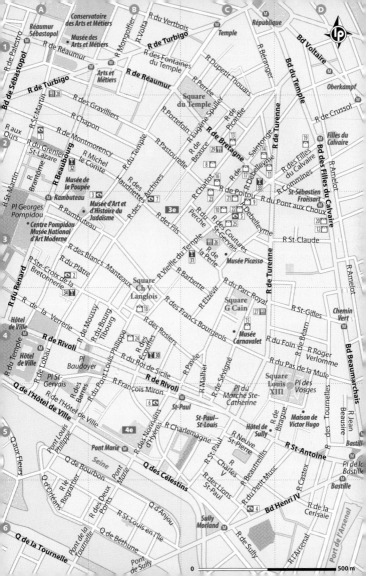

Rue Vieille du Temple, at the heart of Le Marais

◉ SEE

Le Marais is a hive of creativity. Many galleries call it home, making it a must on any tour of contemporary art in the Île de France region. Take a stroll around the Musée Picasso and the Musée d'Art et d'Histoire du Judaïsme (Museum of Jewish Art and History), both housed in superb *hôtels particuliers* (town houses), the Pompidou Centre (p29) and the Rue Debelleyme or Rue Saint-Claude. And don't hesitate to push open any doors to discover what they hide…

◉ MAISON EUROPÉENNE DE LA PHOTOGRAPHIE

☎ 01 44 78 75 00; www.mep-fr.org; 5-7 Rue de Fourcy; full price/concs €6.50/3.50 free entry 5-8pm Wed; ⏰ 11am-8pm Wed-Sun; Ⓜ Saint-Paul or Pont Marie; ♿ Housed in an 18th-century *hôtel particulier*, the museum's excellent

exhibition programme showcasing famous and lesser-known photographers working since the 1950s (including Annie Leibovitz, William Klein, Sophie Elbaz and Peter Knapp), provides an unmissable journey through contemporary art.

◉ GALERIE YVON LAMBERT

☎ 01 42 71 09 33; www.yvon-lambert .com; 108 Rue Vieille du Temple; free entry; ⏰ 10am-1pm & 2.30-7pm Wed-Fri, 10am-7pm Sat; Ⓜ Saint-Sébastien Froissart or Filles du Calvaire
If it's a star of the gallery scene you're after, look no further. For 40 years, Yvon Lambert has been exhibiting international artists to whom he is remarkably loyal, while discovering new creative avenues, notably in video art. His 'stable' includes Nan Goldin, Carl André, Sol Lewitt, Miquel Barcelo, Anselm

FROM GALLERY TO GALLERY

In addition to the galleries mentioned opposite, a number of others are worthy of mention, starting with the American **Marian Goodman** (☎ 01 48 04 70 52; www.mariangoodman .com; 79 Rue du Temple; ☽ 11am-7pm Tue-Sat) for its internationally renowned artists (Dan Graham, Christian Boltanski, Jeff Wall, Annette Messager, Gabriel Orozco) or **Anne de Villepoix** (☎ 01 42 78 32 24; www.annedevillepoix.com; 43 Rue de Montmorency; ☽ 10am-7pm Tue-Sat) for its fine collection of contemporary pieces, including works by photographers, plastic artists, video artists, illustrators (Kader Attia, John Coplans, Huang Yong Ping, Chris Burden). Situated next door to Yvon Lambert (see opposite), the **Galerie Xippas** (☎ 01 40 27 05 55; www.xippas.com; 108 Rue Vieille-du-Temple; ☽ 10am-1pm and 2-7pm Tue-Fri, 10am-7pm Sat) displays paintings, photography, installations and video art, with works by artists such as David Reed, Dan Walsh, Valérie Jouve and Ian Davenport. Don't miss the chance to take the wooden staircase up to the exhibition space. **Beaudoin Lebon** (☎ 01 42 72 09 10; www. baudoin-lebon.com; 38 Rue Sainte-Croix de la Bretonnerie; ☽ 11am-7pm Tue-Sat) is highly diverse, focusing on painting (Jean Dubuffet, Henri Michaux and aboriginal painters), sculpture, installations and photography. The gallery also has an impressive collection of photography from the 19th and 20th centuries. Lastly, photography buffs flock to the **Galerie de l'Agence Vu** (☎ 01 53 01 05 03; www.galerievu.com; 2 Rue Jules Cousin; ☽ 2-7pm Mon-Sat). Situated in the basement, the neon-lit space has an industrial feel and explores reportage and contemplation, as well as the plastic arts. Works by Isabel Muñoz, Lars Tunbjörk and Michael Ackerman have all been exhibited here.

Kieffer, On Kawara, Douglas Gordon, Claude Lévêque and many other talents. A beautiful glass-roofed building.

🅲 MUSÉE DE LA CHASSE ET DE LA NATURE

Museum of Haunting and Nature;
☎ 01 53 01 92 40; www.chassenature
.org; 62 Rue des Archives; full price/concs
€6/4.50; ☽ 11am-6pm Tue-Sun; Ⓜ Hôtel
de Ville or Rambuteau

Who would have believed it? With its completely revamped layout, located in a pair of 17th- and 18th-century town houses, this museum has attracted a whole new generation. Numerous teenagers, armed with sketchbooks, come to copy the posture of an animal or look for inspiration from contemporary artists, such as the dome of owl feathers imagined by Jan Fabre in Diana's cabinet. Covering two main themes, the animal image and the art of hunting, the museum examines mankind's relationship with its natural environment, by inviting contemporary artists to contribute their own vision. A real success!

SHOPPING AND WINDOW SHOPPING

The Upper Marais is teeming with gorgeous boutiques. Hot on the heels of **APC** (112 Rue Vieille du Temple), one of the first to move away from Rue des Francs Bourgeois, a flurry of stores have opened in the district. First the multibrand stores: **Abou d'Abi Bazar** (125 Rue Vieille du Temple), including Madame à Paris, Antik Batik, Isabel Marant Étoile, Iro and Stella Forest; **AB 33** (33 Rue Charlot), in the same romantic vein (Vanessa Bruno, Isabel Marant, See by Chloé), and **Shine** (15 Rue de Poitou), which has a glam rock edge. The boutique **Olga** (103 Rue Vieille du Temple) offers a more unusual collection (Marion Mille, Hache, Thomas Burberry), as does **Dolls** (56 Rue de Saintonge), one of the newest arrivals. As for designers, we like the simple lines of **Ch. Ind** (117 Rue Vieille du Temple) and, conversely, the bright, graphic designs of Greek Cypriot designer **Erotokritos** (109 blvd Beaumarchais), who has launched a more affordable range, Éros. The designers **Vanessa Bruno** (100 Rue Vieille du Temple) and **Isabel Marant** (47 Rue de Saintonge) have also opened up beautiful spaces, as has the ultracreative collective **Surface to Air** (108 Rue Vieille du Temple) which has just produced a collection for the electro duo Justice. To finish on a less expensive note: **L'Habilleur** (44 Rue de Poitou) is the place to go to find designers at knock-down prices. All of these boutiques are usually closed on Sundays and Monday mornings.

 # SHOP

The Rue des Francs Bourgeois, where the boutiques are open on Sundays, has been the place to shop in the Marais district for many years. This is still the case today, but a new shopping enclave has sprung up in the Upper Marais, with the Rue Vieille du Temple, Rue Poitou and Rue Charlot forming a triangle in which delightful fashion and design boutiques, selling their own label wares or those of other brands, have moved.

LES PRAIRIES DE PARIS
Fashion

☎ 01 48 04 91 16; www.lesprairiesdeparis.com; 23 Rue Debelleyme; 🕓 2-7.30pm Mon, 11am-7.30pm Tue-Sat; Ⓜ Filles du Calvaire

At her first shop on the Right Bank, designer Laetitia Ivanez has created an impressive space that falls somewhere between gallery and boutique. Although some of her pieces are used in a *mise-en-scène* on the ground floor, you need to go down to the basement to see the full collection, entrancing with its graphic lines and colours. There is also a small play area for children.

GASPARD YURKIEVICH
Fashion

☎ 01 42 77 42 48; www.gaspard yurkievich.com; 43 Rue Charlot; 🕓 11am-7pm Tue-Sat; Ⓜ Filles du Calvaire

Vibrant creations from Lieu Commun

Avant-garde designer Gaspard Yurkievich draws inspiration from an array of sources. For example, the work of cinematographer Anthony McCall inspires one of his collections. The boutique reflects his sexy urban style: mannequins pose provocatively in the window or lay on the gold-coloured modules that add a decorative touch to the otherwise stark space.

🏠 L'ÉCLAIREUR
Fashion, Design
☎ 01 48 87 10 22; www.leclaireur.com; 40 Rue de Sévigné; 🕙 11am-7pm Mon-Sat; Ⓜ Saint-Paul
Push open the door of the new L'Éclaireur store…not least to admire the wooden sculptures of the artist and designer Arne Quinze. Experience its warm atmosphere

and discover the fabulous ground-breaking work of Martine and Armand Hadida, at the forefront of fashion and design for years now (they had a concept store before concept stores were invented). The Belgian Ann Demeulemeester is among their favourite designers, who also include Undercover and Rick Owens. L'Éclaireur has four other stores in Paris.

🏠 LIEU COMMUN
Fashion, Design
☎ 01 44 54 08 30; www.lieucommun.fr; 5 Rue des Filles du Calvaire; 🕙 11am-1pm and 2-7.30pm Tue-Sat; Ⓜ Filles du Calvaire
This bright blue boutique was opened by three independent creative forces, the designer Matali Crasset, music publisher Blonde Music, and Misericordia, a big name in ethical fashion. Their creations are not merely lined up side-by-side, they interact with each other.

🏠 LES TOURISTES
Fabric, Design
☎ 01 42 72 10 84 ; www.lestouristes.eu; 17 Rue des Blancs Manteaux; 🕙 noon-7pm Tue-Sat; Ⓜ Rambuteau
More than just a shop, this is a world imagined by Yann and Jérôme, two stylists in love with all things Asian and the 1940s. These influences are easy to pick out in their floral fabric creations, which they use to produce

household linen, robes, scarves, bags and an array of unusual objects, all at very reasonable prices.

THE COLLECTION
Design, Interior Decoration
☎ 01 42 77 04 20; www.thecollection.fr; 33 Rue de Poitou; 🕙 noon-7pm; Ⓜ Filles du Calvaire

Limited-edition embroidered or screen-printed wallpaper, *trompe-l'œil* decoration, adhesive friezes to adorn walls, accessories, lights and other decorative objects that defy the run-of-the-mill are sold here. The boutique works with designers such as Dam design, Liz Emtage, Mia Cullin and Suitcase London (for bags). It also produces its own range of products through its line The Collection.

MERCI *Concept Charity Store*
☎ 01 42 77 00 33; www.merci-merci.com; 111 blvd Beaumarchais; 🕙 10am-7pm Mon-Sat; Ⓜ Saint-Sébastien Froissart

Marie-France and Bernard Cohen, formerly of the famous Bonpoint label, have launched a concept store, with the profits being donated to children's charities. Between the Used Book Café on the ground floor and the hip Cantine Merci (☎ 01 42 77 78 92; 🕙 lunch Mon-Sat) on the lower floor, there's 1500 sq metres of shop space to hunt down designer clothes, bunches of fresh flowers,

Annick Goutal perfumes, jewellery, a pair of ballerinas, a trendy pouf, rompers in size 6-months, moleskin notebooks or wooden cutlery. Everything is attractive, elegant and highly original!

TRÉSOR BY *Fashion*
☎ 01 42 72 54 92; 6 Rue du Trésor; 🕙 noon-7.30pm Mon, 11am-7.30pm Tue-Sun; Ⓜ Saint-Paul

Because it is tucked away at the bottom of the Rue de Trésor cul-de-sac, because it is colourful and offers a fantastic selection of young designers at affordable prices, this friendly boutique is one of our absolute favourites.

EAT

The Marais has plenty of tempting little eateries if you can spare a moment between the shops and galleries.

A great place to grab a bite is the **Marché des Enfants Rouges** (39 Rue de Bretagne; 🕙 Tue-Sun), where you can sit outside and enjoy West Indian, Italian or Moroccan food. The Place du Marché Sainte-Catherine, with its many terraces, is a perfect choice when the weather is fine. The falafel sandwiches served in the Rue des Rosiers are an absolute must, even though the street is becoming increasingly overtaken by shops, much to the chagrin of the neighbourhood's residents.

Merci, an ethical and elegant concept store

🍴 APPAREMMENT CAFÉ

Café, Salon de Thé   €

☎ 01 48 87 12 22; 18 Rue des Coutures Saint-Gervais; ⏰ noon-2am Mon-Sat, to midnight Sun; Ⓜ Saint-Sébastien Froissart

Apparemment is a cosy café in which to hang out, with little lamps on the tables, comfy armchairs, wood-clad walls and a wide selection of board games. The menu largely consists of salads and bruschetta. For Sunday brunch, anything goes (you tick the ingredients that you want on a check list). This is an option to bear in mind for bad weather days or during the winter, when there is barely any natural light.

🍴 CAFÉ DES MUSÉES

Modern Bistro   €€

☎ 01 42 72 96 17; 49 Rue de Turenne; ⏰ 8am-midnight; Ⓜ Chemin Vert

This modern bistro is a pleasant surprise. If you are seated in the front room (the smallest), you will be able to see the chefs bustling around in the tiny kitchen, cutting and cooking the fine cuts of meat. The lunch menu is particularly interesting.

🍴 DERRIÈRE

French   €€€

☎ 01 44 61 91 95; 69 Rue des Gravilliers; ⏰ lunch Tue-Fri, dinner Tue-Sun; Ⓜ Arts et Métiers

This address is already very famous and popular with celebrities, just *derrière* the no less famous 404. It's the same management, but with a very different atmosphere: here, you are at home! Once inside the apartment, you just need to choose the room in which you'd like to eat (the lounge, boudoir, or bedroom), the atmosphere (a cosy corner or a large family table), all in a somewhat haphazard décor, yet not overdone – just like at home, really. The restaurant features slow-cooked food (leg of lamb, ox cheek, spit-roasted ham) that does not disappoint.

NEIGHBOURHOODS

LE MARAIS

🍴 USAGI *Japanese* €€€
☎ 01 48 87 28 85; 58 Rue de Saintonge;
⏰ dinner Mon-Sat; Ⓜ Filles du Calvaire
A modern and ultra-trendy
restaurant – right down to the plates
and bentos (lunch boxes) – fusioning
Japanese and French influences.
Apparently usagi is Japanese for
"rabbit". You will understand why if
you visit the toilets…

🍸 DRINK
There is no shortage of terraces
and cafés in the Marais, which has
equal numbers of gay (particularly
on the Rue des Archives) and
straight venues.

🍸 3W KAFÉ *Gay & Lesbian Bar*
☎ 01 48 87 39 26; www.3w-kafe.com;
8 Rue des Écouffes; ⏰ 5pm-2am, to 4am
Fri & Sat; Ⓜ Hôtel de Ville
3W is a lesbian bar. Men are
welcome, but few and far between
at this cosy Marais venue. DJs spin
on Fridays and Saturdays.

🍸 LA PERLE *Café*
☎ 01 42 72 69 93; 78 Rue Vieille du
Temple; ⏰ 6am-2am Mon-Fri,
8am-2am Sat & Sun; Ⓜ Chemin Vert
Long before the boutiques arrived
en masse at the top of the Rue
Vieille du Temple, Jean-Philippe
had already taken over this
neighbourhood café without
changing the décor, quickly

attracting a trendy crowd thrilled by
its authenticity. It is a great place to
meet for pre-dinner drinks.

🍸 ANDY WAHLOO *Bar*
☎ 01 42 71 20 38; 69 Rue des Gravilliers;
⏰ 6pm-2am Tue-Sat; Ⓜ Arts et Métiers
Adjacent to the Derrière (p103),
this bar, whose décor manages to
combine Warholian pop art with
oriental style, is a perfect place to
enjoy a drink and snack or, when a
DJ is playing, to dance till you drop.

🍸 LE PROGRÈS *Café*
☎ 01 42 72 01 44; 1 Rue de Bretagne;
⏰ 8am-10pm Mon-Sat; Ⓜ Saint-
Sébastien Froissart
Le Progrès is a calmer, more
traditional version of La Perle.
This handsome café with art deco
ceramics was at one time a popular
haunt of the American writers known
as the 'Lost Generation'. It is the
ideal spot to have a daytime drink or
enjoy lunch. The terrace is perfectly
situated for people-watching.

🍸 LE DUPLEX *Gay Bar*
☎ 01 42 72 80 86; 25 Rue Michel Lecomte;
⏰ 8pm-2am, to 4am Fri & Sat;
Ⓜ Rambuteau
This arty Parisian gay bar is both
an exhibition space and a convivial
meeting place, whose enduring
popularity means that it is always
packed on the weekend.

>BELLEVILLE AND MÉNILMONTANT: HOME TO A NEW WAVE OF BOHEMIANS

Off the well-trodden tourist trail, Belleville and Ménilmontant exude a young and arty feel that is refreshingly unpretentious and well worth investigating. This involves a steep climb up streets named after past luminaries before you are immersed in the atmosphere unique to the neighbourhood. This village part of the capital is a place to party or relax: the city centre seems far away and residents often say they are 'going down' to Paris. You have a real sense of history when wandering around the buttresses in the Parc des Buttes Chaumont or exploring narrow, winding streets, before heading onto the buzzing Boulevard de Belleville and the Oberkampf district. This old working-class neighbourhood, where Édith Piaf was allegedly born on a pavement in 1915, has been adopted by immigrants from North Africa and China. Now the *bobos* (bourgeois bohemians) are moving in and hoards of artists have set up here. A host of bars has also opened, reflecting the mood of this swinging, bohemian area.

BELLEVILLE AND MÉNILMONTANT

See map on following page

SEE

PARC DE BELLEVILLE
☎ 01 43 28 47 63; 27 Rue Piat; free entry; ☼ park opens at sunrise and closes at sunset; Maison de l'Air 1.30-5.30pm Tue-Fri, to 6.30pm Sat & Sun Apr-Sep, 1.30-5.30pm Tue-Sun Oct-Mar, to 5pm Nov-Feb M Pyrénées or Couronnes
From the vineyard at the top of the Parc de Belleville, you will be treated to one of the best views that Paris has to offer. This little-known park that covers 4.5 hectares is landscaped to form terraces. Early in the morning, Chinese residents can be seen practising t'ai chi on the top slopes. The park is also home to the Maison de l'Air hosting a permanent exhibition on air and environmental issues. In summer, droves of people from all backgrounds come to relax on the grass and free concerts are sometimes organised.

LE PLATEAU
☎ 01 53 19 84 10; www.fracidf-leplateau.com; Place Hannah Arendt, cnr Rue des Alouettes & Rue Carducci; free entry; ☼ 2-7pm Wed-Fri, noon-8pm Sat & Sun; M Buttes Chaumont; ♿
This contemporary art space is a touch austere but benefits from large windows looking out onto the surrounding streets. There are four exhibitions that are held each year, one of which displays the collection of the Île-de-France FRAC (Regional Fund of Contemporary Art). An experimental area presents the work of several artists, including Keren Cytter, Corey McCorkle and Charles Avery.

MAISON DES MÉTALLOS
☎ 01 48 05 88 27; www.maisondesmetallos.org; 94 Rue Jean-Pierre Timbaud; free entry, shows full price/concs €13/9; ☼ 10am-7pm Mon-Fri, 2-7pm Sat, to 10pm Sun & show nights; M Couronnes; ♿
This headquarters of the Paris trade-union movement is being given a new life. Located in an old industrial building that has been restored to its former glory, a new cultural project has taken hold. The Maison is a centre for disciplines as diverse as dance, performance, the

A panoramic view of Paris from the Parc de Belleville

BELLEVILLE ART TOUR

Don't be afraid to pry when checking out the art scene in Belleville! If you're walking down the Rue Denoyez for instance, make sure you take a detour to see the alternative artists' squat known as La Miroiterie at number 88 Rue de Ménilmontant if the door's not locked or take a look at the **Jérôme Mesnager** famous white men, which pirouette across a wooden building designed by Philippe Madec on the corner of the Rue de la Duée and an alley with the same name. Cinema fans should head to the Villa Castel at 16 Rue du Transvaal where François Truffaut filmed some of the scenes from *Jules et Jim* and 44 Rue des Cascades where Jacques Becker's *Casque d'Or* was filmed (although you have to use your imagination here).

The best time to see art in the neighbourhood is in May when the galleries open to the public. This is the chance for the 250 artists in Belleville to open their studios for four days of festivities, allowing visitors to see over 130 work and living spaces. The organisation **Les Ateliers d'Artistes de Belleville** (www.ateliers-artistes-belleville.org) which organises the event has a permanent base in a gallery (32 Rue de la Mare) exhibiting work from local artists. **Les Ateliers d'Artistes de Ménilmontant** (http://ateliersdemenilmontant. org), an artists' collective in Ménilmontant also opens its studios to the public in September.

Finally, don't miss the **Galerie Suzanne Tarasiève** (☎ 01 45 86 02 02; www.suzanne-tarasieve.com; Passage de l'Atlas, 5 Villa Marcel-Lods; Ⓜ Belleville),which closely follows German artists, or **La Vitrine** (☎ 01 43 38 49 65; www.ensapc.fr/lavitrine; 24 Rue Moret; Ⓜ Couronnes or Ménilmontant), the exhibition area of the Paris-Cergy National Art School.

living arts, plastic arts and digital arts. Studio space is also available for amateurs. There is a pleasant café on the mezzanine level.

🗀 SHOP

All the different communities in Belleville rub shoulders at the market every Tuesday and Friday morning on the Boulevard de Belleville, where stalls overflow with fruits, vegetables, spices, condiments and African, Middle Eastern and Asian food. Local artists also sell their work here.

🗀 POLLEN *Fashion*

☎ 01 42 02 31 20; 7 Rue de la Villette;
🕑 11am-2pm & 3.30-7pm Tue-Sat;
Ⓜ Jourdain

This friendly boutique offers a fine selection of designer clothes, jewellery and shoes at reasonable prices. Check out the crochet chair and wallpaper designed by Aurélie Mathigot.

🗀 LIBRAIRIE PHOTOGRAPHIQUE *Bookshop*

☎ 01 48 07 80 90; 17 Rue de la Villette;
🕑 11am-1pm & 3-7.30pm Wed-Sat, to 7pm Sun; Ⓜ Jourdain

Belleville and Ménilmontant – a place of free artistic expression

Marc, a former photographic agent, now shares his passion for photos and photography books in this bookshop where he is more than happy to look at the different works with you because in his mind a picture is worth a thousand words. He also organises exhibitions, including an annual show featuring the pinhole camera (an optical device based on the camera obscura).

⬠ ATELIER BEAU TRAVAIL
Fashion Showroom
www.beautravail.fr; 67 Rue de la Mare; ⏲ 2.30-7.30pm Sat or by appointment; Ⓜ Jourdain
Four young female designers have joined forces to make clothes, handbags, lights and other fun items. They share this white-tiled studio in Ménilmontant which is open to the

public on Saturday afternoons and for themed exhibitions.

🍴 EAT
In Belleville and the surrounding area, you can enjoy the full spectrum of world cuisine, often available at reasonable prices and without having to book. When walking around you will see African, Thai, Korean, Japanese, Chinese, Indian as well as other types of restaurants intermingled with more traditional French bistros.

🍴 LE BARIOLÉ *Café* €
☎ 01 42 49 17 33; 103 Rue de Belleville; ⏲ 7.30am-2am Mon-Fri, 8.30am-9pm Sun; Ⓜ Jourdain
One of the neighbourhood's gems which is great for lunch. The décor is typical of a Parisian bistro with

bay windows which are opened at the first sign of sun to provide a breath of fresh air from the street. Traditional food is offered, with steaks served on wooden boards.

L'AUTRE CAFÉ *Café* €

☎ 01 40 21 03 07; www.lautrecafe .com; 62 Rue Jean-Pierre Timbaud; ⏰ 8am-2am Mon-Sat, 9am-2am Sun; Ⓜ Parmentier

This large café with a mezzanine floor is a perfect place to relax. Exhibitions of local artists are displayed on the walls and tasty traditional food is served. Sunday brunch and wi-fi access.

L'ESCARGOT
Bar-Restaurant €€

☎ 01 42 06 03 96; 50 Rue de la Villette; ⏰ 5pm-2am Tue-Sat; Ⓜ Jourdain

A colourful and friendly bar-restaurant popular with the locals. Besides a gargantuan cocktail list featuring over 150 drinks, the menu has some surprises in store such as the pan-fried foie gras with hibiscus sauce for starters and delicious mains including kangaroo fillet.

CHAPEAU MELON
Table d'Hôtes €€

☎ 01 42 02 68 60; 92 Rue Rébeval; ⏰ from 8.30pm Wed-Sat, Sun evening à la carte ; Ⓜ Pyrénées

The Chapeau Melon stands out among all the restaurants on the

La Rôtisserie, a place for locals to cook up new ideas

Rue Rébeval. Resident cellarman and organic wine specialist Olivier Camus invites guests to take a seat at his intimate *table d'hôtes* with room for only 12 diners to enjoy his delicious creations. There is a set menu with four savoury courses. Bookings are compulsory.

MAMA SHELTER
Fusion €€€

☎ 01 43 48 48 48; www.mamashelter .com; 109 Rue de Bagnolet; ⏰ restaurant daily, bar daily 6pm-2am; Ⓜ Alexandre Dumas or Porte-de-Bagnolet

The designer Philip Starck is the genius behind his new ultratrendy place (hotel, bar and restaurant), with Alain Senderens in charge in the kitchen. The setting is in a

THE VILLAGE SAINTE-MARTHE

It's easy to miss the little pocket of activity around the Rue Sainte-Marthe and the Place Sainte-Marthe, home to a multitude of artists. Off the beaten track, it is reminiscent of a village and maintains a truly grass-roots feel and community spirit – but for how much longer? The **Rôtisserie** (☎ 01 40 03 08 30; www.larotisserie.org; 4 Rue Sainte-Marthe), a restaurant funding community projects, is typical of the area but under threat of closure. Bars and restaurants with colourful façades dot the Rue Sainte-Marthe including **Jambo** (☎ 01 42 45 46 55; 23 Rue Sainte-Marthe) a lovely Rwandan restaurant with an excellent reputation. The picturesque Place Sainte-Marthe offers a change of scenery with its overflowing terraces and cafés, including the **Sainte-Marthe** (☎ 01 44 84 36 96; 🕑 5pm-2am Mon-Sat, 2pm-2am Sun), which has been here for years.

modern building on the edge of the Petite Ceinture, opposite La Flèche d'Or (p113), with mirrors and a surreal décor. The cuisine is simple and authentic (soft-boiled egg and asparagus emulsion à la kalamata, caramelised chicken with coriander). There is brunch on Sundays and a DJ from Thursday to Saturday.

🍴 CHEZ VINCENT *Italian*   €€€
☎ 01 42 02 22 45; opposite 43 Av Simon Bolivar; 🕑 dinner Mon-Sat; Ⓜ Buttes Chaumont

Vincent has traded in his little trattoria for a rococo-style restaurant in the Parc des Buttes Chaumont – the Pavillon Pueblo. The set menus from €30 to €50 are admittedly not cheap, but the quality is beyond reproach and the terrace alone is worth a trip on sunny days. The tearoom is open in the afternoons.

🍴 LA BOULANGERIE
Modern Bistro   €€€
☎ 01 43 58 45 45; 15 Rue des Panoyaux; 🕑 lunch & dinner Tue-Fri, dinner only Sat; Ⓜ Ménilmontant

Opposite the Lou Pascalou (p112), this modern bistro in an old bakery provides a dream setting with chandeliers, red seats – the works. The food is sophisticated with a wine list for refined palates.

🍴 LE CHATEAUBRIAND
Gastropub   €€€€
☎ 01 43 57 45 95; 129 Av Parmentier; 🕑 dinner Tue-Sat; Ⓜ Goncourt

Since Basque chef Iñaki Aizpitarte (see p115) took over this bistro, you need to reserve at least a week in advance to stand a chance of sampling the set menu featuring a meal in five or six stages, juxtaposing flavours, as with the cheeky suckling veal and beetroot with smoked herrings. There are plans to take over an annex

EASTERN DELIGHTS

The neighbourhood is brimming with Asian restaurants. Here are two which won't let you down. The Thai restaurant **Reuan Thaï** (☎ 01 43 55 15 82; 36 Rue de l'Orillon) serves delicate dishes with a huge selection of delicious salads and main courses in a pleasant setting. For more sensitive pallets, there are symbols on the menu indicating how spicy the food is. The Vietnamese restaurant **Cyclo** (☎ 01 40 33 48 86; 78 Rue de Belleville) also serves great food and you'll be forgiven for spoiling yourself with one of their scrumptious desserts. Reservations are recommended for both restaurants.

called Le Dauphin with simple, local food at lunchtime and tapas in the evening.

DRINK

Besides the Rue Oberkampf and its many bars, there are a number of cafés dotted around Belleville and Ménilmontant. Some have not changed in years while others have been studiously refurbished to retain a certain rundown feel – they are bohemian hangouts after all!

Y CAFÉ CHARBON *Café*

☎ 01 43 57 55 13; 109 Rue Oberkampf; 9am-2am Sun-Wed, to 4am Thu-Sat; Ⓜ Parmentier

The Café Charbon opened the flood gates for a wave of trendy cafés on the Rue Oberkampf and remains a focal point. A delicious brunch is served on Sundays in an airy room with high ceilings and seating reminiscent of an old train carriage. There's a party atmosphere in the evenings.

Y CAFÉ CHÉRI(E) *Bar*

☎ 01 42 02 02 05; www.cafecherie .blogspot.com; 44 blvd de la Villette; 11.30am-2am Mon-Fri, from 11am Sat and 1pm Sun; Ⓜ Belleville

A great place to go before hitting a club with electro, punch and red lighting. The terrace is superb in summer.

Y LOU PASCALOU *Bar*

☎ 01 46 38 78 10; www.myspace.com/ leloupascalou; 14 Rue des Panoyaux; 9am-2am; Ⓜ Ménilmontant

This large, bright café, extended by a large shady terrace, is highly popular in the summer. Service is simple and friendly. Occasional exhibitions and live music in the evenings.

Y LE CANNIBALE *Bar*

☎ 01 49 29 95 59; www.myspace.com/ lecannibalecafe; 93 Rue Jean-Pierre Timbaud; 8am-2am Mon-Fri, from 9am Sat & Sun; Ⓜ Couronnes

This no-frills bar with a fine zinc counter and a long room crowded with benches and beaten-up chairs is a favourite. The terrace is great for pre-dinner drinks. A varied programme is offered: mix session on Fridays and Saturdays, live music on Sundays and some Tuesday evenings.

⭐ PLAY

⭐ LE CAFÉ DES SPORTS
Music Venue

☎ 01 46 36 48 18; www.myspace.com/lecafedessports; 94 Rue de Ménilmontant; free entry; 🕙 11am-2am every day; Ⓜ Ménilmontant or Gambetta

There is live music every night in this bar which features a eclectic line-up of rock, funk, electro, hip-hop, French *chanson* (song music), jazz, reggae... DJs Friday and Saturday evening with a small dance floor, world music on Thursdays and jazz on Sundays.

⭐ LA FLÈCHE D'OR
Live Music Venue, Club

☎ 01 44 64 01 02; www.flechedor.fr; 102 bis Rue de Bagnolet; concerts €8; 🕙 7.30pm-2am, to 6am Thu-Sat; Ⓜ Gambetta or Alexandre Dumas

Opposite the Mama Shelter (p110), this venue is unusual both in terms of the building, an old train station with a slightly underground feel, and its line-up of live music with four gigs per night, featuring bands from the new indie scene and club nights. (see the programme on the internet).

⭐ LA JAVA *Live Music Venue, Club*

☎ 01 42 02 20 52; www.la-java.fr; 105 Rue du Faubourg du Temple; €5-15; 🕙 concerts from 8.30pm Wed-Fri, club from 11pm Fri & Sat; Ⓜ Belleville or Goncourt

This is the ballroom where Edith Piaf started out and Django Reinhardt first plied his brand of gypsy jazz. These days it puts on world music, electro, rock, French *chanson* (song) and salsa nights with a DJ.

Le Baxo, an urban lounge (p114)

NEIGHBOURHOODS

BELLEVILLE AND MÉNILMONTANT

⭐ LE NOUVEAU CASINO
Live Music Venue, Club

☎ 01 43 57 57 40; www.nouveau casino.net; 109 Rue Oberkampf; entry free-€25; 🕑 concerts from 7pm, club 11pm-dawn; Ⓜ Parmentier

Kitsch décor with baroque touches, great acoustics and an eclectic line-up including small-scale gigs, DJs from around the world, electro, pop, deep house and rock make the Casino a hip place to be.

⭐ LA BELLEVILLOISE
Live Music Venue, Club

☎ 01 46 36 07 07; www.labellevilloise .com; 19-21 Rue Boyer; entry free-€25; 🕑 7pm-2am Wed & Thu, 6pm-2am Fri, 11am-1am Sun; Ⓜ Gambetta or Ménilmontant

The management of this historic venue, established after the Paris Commune in 1871 (La Bellevilloise was the first Parisian cooperative), sprawls over several floors and has kept its independent spirit alive while diversifying into a variety of different areas. There are exhibitions, fashion shows, debates, club nights and live music. The Sunday brunch with live music and the charming little terrace, which closes at 11pm, are very popular.

⭐ LA MAROQUINERIE
Live Music Venue

☎ 01 40 33 35 05; www.myspace.com .lamaroquinerie; 23 Rue Boyer; €18-20;

🕑 gigs at 7pm or 8pm, bar 6pm-2am; Ⓜ Ménilmontant

Next to La Bellevilloise, this old tannery is now a small music venue which never ceases to amaze with a line-up consisting mainly of modern and rock music, so it's always worth dropping in to see what's on. The venue offers a bar-restaurant and a small courtyard which opens in summer. There are also occasional club nights and a literary café.

⭐ BAXO *Club*

☎ 01 42 02 99 71; www.baxo.fr; free entry; 21 Rue Juliette Dodu; 🕑 9am-3pm & 5pm-2am; Ⓜ Colonel Fabien

From Thursday to Saturday night, this colourful and stylish urban lounge plays host to underground musicians including DJs such as Patrick Vidal and DJ Deep with a heavy emphasis on electro. There is a tiny dance floor and seating in the courtyard for sunny days.

⭐ ROSA BONHEUR *Bar, Club*

www.myspace.com/rosabonheurparis; Parc des Buttes Chaumont, 2 Allée de la Cascade (entrance via 7 rue Botzaris); 🕑 to midnight Wed-Sun; Ⓜ Botzaris

Nestled in a little hunting lodge inside the Parc des Buttes Chaumont, the Rosa guarantees a great time with its festive atmosphere, along with dance sets mixed by former Pulp DJs.

Iñaki Aizpitarte,
Chef at Le Chateaubriand (p111)

You are well-known for the freedom of expression in your cuisine… I like unusual combinations and I try to analyse the taste, while letting my imagination express itself. I am guided by the seasons – in early spring, I choose the first asparagus and young sorrel leaves or wild watercress that I then serve with citrus fruits or squid. **How has Le Chateaubriand been a change for you?** Here I can cook the way I like in a low-key place and with a relaxed service. I'd had enough of the protocol of famous restaurants. I now feel closer to the people. What we call bistronomie is above all a way of being. **You originally come from the Basque country. What do you like about Paris?** The mix of people – I spend most of my time in the east of Paris which is still pretty much working class. I live near the Canal Saint-Martin, I work a little further up and I often go across the upper reaches of Belleville. **What are your favourite places?** Le Verre Volé (p58), a wine-seller who really knows his trade and also delights his customers, and Le Baratin for Raquel's cooking which is fabulous. Like everyone else, I also have my favourite Chinese restaurant in the Rue de Belleville, Le Wenzhou.

Le Baratin: 01 43 49 39 70; 3 Rue Jouye-Rouve, 20th
Le Wenzhou: 01 46 36 56 33; 24 Rue de Belleville, 20th

>MONTMARTRE, BARBÈS, SAINT-OUEN AND SAINT-DENIS: GRASS-ROOTS PARIS

Thanks to the current urban regeneration project, north-eastern Paris is undergoing a transformation. Prior to the construction of the Stade de France sports stadium in Saint-Denis, Parisians barely ventured into this district other than to visit the Saint-Ouen flea markets. A few years earlier, a trendy bar-hotel like the Ice Kube would have been unimaginable in a working-class area like La Chapelle. So things are changing. Often community-based, centres of creativity and dissemination are integrated into urban culture and breathe life into the neighbourhoods. Le Café Culturel in Saint-Denis, for example, is a springboard for slam artists, Mains d'Œuvres in Saint-Ouen is a centre of exploration and discovery open to the public, while L'Olympic Café and Le Lavoir Moderne Parisien are the *enfants terribles* of the Goutte d'Or district.

MONTMARTRE, BARBÈS, SAINT-OUEN, SAINT-DENIS

📷 SEE

Basilique de Saint-Denis...	1	G1
Espace Canopy...	2	H5
Espace Synesthésie ...	3	G1
Galerie Christine Diegoni...	4	D6
Halle Saint-Pierre...	5	E6
Jardin Saint-Vincent ...	6	D5
Musée Pierre Cardin...	7	A2
Saint-Ouen Flea Markets...	8	D1
Stade de France...	9	H2
Villa Léandre ...	10	D5

🛍 SHOP

Atelier Franciade...	11	G1
Emmanuelle Zysman...	12	D6
French Touche ...	13	B5
Guerrisol...	14	F6
Lilly Lafiti ...	15	F6
Marcia de Carvalho ...	16	F6
Rue Houdon...	17	D6
Saint-Denis Market ...	18	G1
Sakina M'sa ...	(See 16)	
Spree ...	19	D6
Tati...	20	F6

🍴 EAT

Cafe Burq...	21	D5
Chez Serge...	22	B1
Chez Toinette ...	23	D6
La Famille ...	24	D6
Le Bouclard...	25	B5
Le Picolo ...	26	D2
Le P'tit Landais...	27	D1

🍷 DRINK

Au Rendez-Vous des Amis...	28	D6
Café Culturel...	29	H1
Chez Nadjet...	30	G6
Ice Kube ...	31	G5
La Cave Café...	32	D4
La Chope des Puces...	33	E1
La Fourmi ...	34	D6
Olympic Café ...	35	G5

⭐ PLAY

Centre Musical Barbara...	36	G6
Élysée-Montmartre...	37	E6
Le Divan du Monde...	38	D6
Les Trois Baudets...	39	C6
Mains d'Oeuvres...	40	D1

See map on following pages

Next door, Montmartre may seem overrun, but there is more to it than tourist crowds. Designers, galleries, bars and live-music venues have made space for themselves and continue to feed the bohemian party spirit of La Butte.

◉ SEE

Don't let the imposing figures of the Sacré-Cœur and the Basilique de Saint-Denis overshadow the other sites that help form the cultural and urban landscape of northeastern Paris, at once cutting edge and grass-roots.

◉ MONTMARTRE'S HIDDEN GEMS

Montmartre is not summed up by *Amélie*, even if you will no doubt be reminded of the heroine of the film directed by Jean-Pierre Jeunet. It would be a shame to limit your visit to the Sacré-Cœur, Rue des Abbesses or Rue Lepic, when peace and tranquillity can be found walking along **Avenue Junot**, one of the most expensive streets in Paris. Here you'll find its **Villa Léandre**, accessed via number 23 bis, a very British-looking cul-de-sac with coloured-brick houses. Just before the Villa, at number 23, a gate allows you to see a strange stone called 'Rocher de la Sorcière' (the witch's stone), a relic from the Montmartre scrubland. The crudely paved lane also leads to a stylish and discreet (unmarked) hotel, the **Hôtel Particulier de Montmartre** (23 Av Junot; www.hotel-particulier-montmartre.com). Another option is to take the romantic **Allée des Brouillards** which starts at Place Dalida and

A colourful boutique on the streets of Montmartre

leads to Place Casadesus, from which you can take Rue Simon Dereure to rejoin Avenue Junot. When you reach **Rue Caulaincourt**, you leave the clichéd Montmartre of the Haut de la Butte. Don't miss the opportunity to walk behind the Place de Clichy, between Avenue de Clichy and the Montmartre Cemetery. The peaceful alleyways and cul-de-sacs provide welcome relief and hide away some architectural treasures. One last secret place, so fragile it is only open to the public on Saturdays between April and October, is the **Jardin Sauvage Saint-Vincent** (10am-12.30pm & 1.30pm-6pm, to 6.30pm Apr-Sep). Located opposite 14 Rue Saint-Vincent, this 1480-sq-metre garden, which also features a

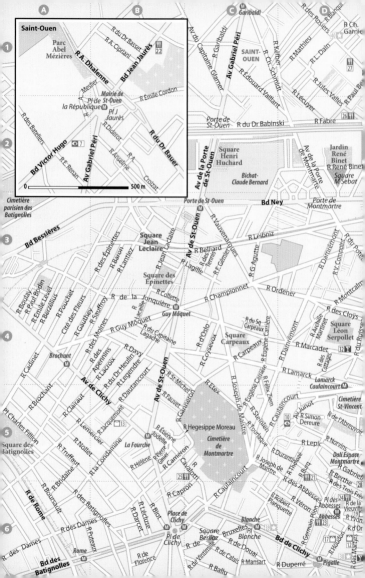

pond, has been colonised by a wide variety of wild flora and fauna.

HALLE SAINT-PIERRE

☎ 01 42 58 72 89; www.hallesaintpierre .org; 2 Rue Ronsard; full-price/concs €7.50/6; ⏰ 10am-6pm daily, noon-6pm Mon-Fri Aug; Ⓜ Abbesses or Anvers

This fine Baltard-style building is devoted to outsider art – otherwise known as 'the hidden face of contemporary art'. Large exhibits and monographs follow one after the other, inviting the public into a world that is dreamlike, and occasionally hallucinatory and/or filled with poetry. After exhibitions such as 'Oh la Vache', 'Civilisations Imaginaires' and 'British Outsider Art', the Halle Saint-Pierre displayed the work of over 60 Japanese outsider artists. There is also a gallery, a bookshop and a pleasant café, together with sessions and workshops that are run for the young.

GALERIE CHRISTINE DIEGONI

☎ 01 42 64 69 48; www.christinediegoni .fr; 47 ter Rue d'Orsel; free entry; ⏰ 2-7pm Tue-Fri, 11am-7pm Sat; Ⓜ Pigalle

Fans of the furniture and lighting of the 1930s, 1950s and 1970s flock to this elegant gallery that has displayed the work of Gino Sarfatti, George Nelson, Charles and Ray Eames, among many other designers.

ESPACE CANOPY

☎ 06 06 72 26 67; www.labelette.info; 19 Rue Pajol; free entry; ⏰ 2-7.30pm Wed-Fri, to 7pm Sat; Ⓜ La Chapelle, Gare du Nord or Marx Dormoy

Its raspberry-red façade is hard to miss. Initially set up to display the works of little-known artists and to build bridges between disciplines, this bright and gorgeous gallery also organises other events, such as poetry and 'slam' nights on the third Friday of the month.

ESPACE SYNESTHÉSIE

☎ 01 40 10 80 78; www.synesthesie .com; 15 Rue Denfert-Rochereau, Saint-Denis; free entry; ⏰ 2-6pm Tue-Sat during exhibitions or by appointment; Ⓜ Saint-Denis Porte de Paris or RER D Saint-Denis

A pioneer in the arena of inter-disciplinary digital art, until recently the Synesthésie association only existed on the internet, where a virtual art centre displays contemporary works specially designed on and for the web. A real exhibition space now exists, where the works are displayed and the virtual meets the actual.

STADE DE FRANCE

☎ 0892 70 09 00; www.stadefrance.com; Rue Francis de Pressensé, ZAC du Cornillon Nord, Saint-Denis La Plaine; guided tour full price/concs/under 6 yrs €12/8/free; ⏰ daily except events days, closed on Mon outside of school holidays, tours every hour 10am-5pm (in English at 10.30am & 2.30pm); M Saint-Denis Porte de Paris or RER B and D Stade de France

The most striking aspects of the stadium are its sheer scale, the open roof (supported by pylons and cables on the outside of the terraces, it appears to hover above the crowd) and its versatility (the first few rows are retractable and hide an athletics track). Built in record time for the 1998 World Soccer Cup, it was soon embraced by the Saint-Denis locals, doubtless partly thanks to the French team's victory that year. The hour-long, highly comprehensive guided tours are the only way to see the stadium outside of the sporting, musical and other events held there.

SAINT-OUEN FLEA MARKETS

☎ 01 40 11 77 36 guided tours; www .marchesauxpuces.fr; ☺ 9am-6pm Sat, 10am-6pm Sun, 10am-5pm Mon; M Porte de Clignancourt or Garibaldi

Saint-Ouen owes its national and international fame to its markets. There are around 15 of them, all very different in terms of organisation and history, as well as their style and the items on sale. A project is underway to make the *puces* (flea markets) more attractive and accessible. Soak up the atmosphere walking through the labyrinthine stalls and take the time to enjoy a coffee or relaxed meal.

The main markets are the **Marché Vernaison** (Rue des Rosiers and 136 Avenue Michelet), with its wide range of items

WHERE TO EAT AND DRINK AT THE PUCES

Le Picolo (☎ 01 40 11 11 19; www.lepicolo.com; 58 Rue Jules Vallès; ☺ bar/restaurant 9am-7pm Sat-Mon & show nights). This restaurant dates back to the first days of the flea market, or thereabouts. Come here for big helpings of home-style cooking, using high-quality seasonal produce. The large room is furnished with wooden tables and an upright piano, and there is a charming terrace among the market stalls. The restaurant is a venue for live music on weekend nights and comedy during the week.

La Chope des Puces (☎ 01 40 11 02 49; www.lachopedespuces.com; 122 Rue des Rosiers; ☺ Wed-Mon). A small old-style café. This legendary gypsy-jazz haunt showcases live music almost every weekend, with artists including Thomas Dutronc, Mondine and Ninine Garcia, among others.

Le P'tit Landais (☎ 01 49 45 11 55; 96 Rue des Rosiers; ☺ Fri-Mon 8am-8pm). Very simple fare cooked to order. Salads, grilled meat, sausages and chips and produce from the Landes region (foie gras is on sale here). Service with a smile. The outdoor tables are highly coveted when the sun shines. Live music on Sunday afternoons.

(antique dolls, 18th-century crystal glasses, old postcards, hatpins, miniature cars) and open-air café Chez Louisette; the **Marché Biron** (85 Rue des Rosiers), whose gangways form a large square devoted to the art and decorative arts of the 20th century, crystal glassware, furniture, paintings, brassware and lighting. In a modern building on the opposite side of the street, the **Marché Dauphine** (140 Rue des Rosiers) sells valuable furniture and objects to collectors. Don't miss the booksellers' square (antique books, comic strips, children's books and much more). The walk takes on a more relaxed air in the **Marché Paul Bert** (96 Rue Paul Bert) where stalls are arranged like living rooms.

Every year the **Festival Jazz-Musette des Puces** (www.festivaldespuces.com), from the end of June to early July, and the **Mondial de l'Antiquité** in October make the markets jive.

MUSÉE PIERRE CARDIN
☎ 01 49 21 08 20; www.pierrecardin .com; 33 blvd Victor Hugo, Saint-Ouen; full price/concs €15/12; 2-5pm Wed & Sat & Sun ; M Mairie de Saint-Ouen
Pierre Cardin chose this old glass-roofed garage in Saint-Ouen to create his loft-style museum. More than 130 mannequins show off the couturier's creations from various periods, the most striking of which is probably his cosmos period from 1965 to 1970.

 # SHOP

Over the space of a few years, clothes shops have overtaken the Rue des Abbesses, often to the detriment of food outlets. Brands flourishing elsewhere can now be found here. However, you just need to venture off the main street into the side roads to find more creative places. Barbès still heads the field in low-cost fashion lines, with key names including Tati, Sympa and Guerrisol.

SPREE
Fashion, Design
☎ 01 42 23 41 40; www.spree.fr; 16 Rue de la Vieuville; 11am-7.30pm Tue-Sat, 3-7pm Sun & Mon; M Abbesses
This gorgeous boutique-gallery manages to offer an edgy range, without detracting from its warm atmosphere. Clothes and accessories designers including Tsumori Chisato, Giulia Persanti, Preen, Avril Gau and Jérôme Dreyfus feature. For furniture and lighting, the style recalls the 1950s through to the 1980s. Artists are also regularly exhibited in the front room.

EMMANUELLE ZYSMAN
Fashion
☎ 01 42 52 01 00; www.emmanuelle zysman.fr; 81 Rue des Martyrs; 11am-7pm Tue-Fri, noon-8pm Sat, 3.30-7pm Sun; M Abbesses or Pigalle

Sakina M'sa,
Fashion designer at La Goutte-d'Or (see the boxed text p124)

How does a 'Parisienne' dress? Paris women are audacious, inventing their own look with elegance and a touch of avant-garde. **How do you dress them?** I draw inspiration from the cuts of the famous couturiers, such as Chanel, Balenciaga or Worth, adding a futurist touch which is more relevant to our age which is not kind on today's women. I would like my clothes to give them a degree of grace. **Your collection tends towards 'haute couture'...** Designing and making clothes is slow, behind-the-scenes work, involving modesty and yet it's their 'skin' that the *couturier* displays on the catwalk every six months. Another aspect that I believe is really important is that all my clothes are made in my workshop. Admittedly, the cost is higher, but this also creates better life values. **Where can we find your designs?** In my workshop-boutique or on my website. People who are interested can also sign up for my customisation workshops, where we work on both imaginary designs and with real fabrics. **Which places inspire you in Paris?** The major Grand Palais exhibitions, together with the collections of the Dapper and Cernuschi museums, with tea ceremonies that are also perfect for an energy boost. But to drink a Goutte-d'Or mint tea, go to Chez Nadjet, where they also do a delicious couscous!

Chez Nadjet (ex-Goutte Rouge): 01 42 54 02 55; 19 Rue Polonceau, 18th
Grand Palais: 01 44 13 17 17; www.grandpalais.fr; Av Winston Churchill, 8th
Musée Dapper: 01 45 00 91 75; www.dapper.com; 35 Rue Paul Valéry, 16th
Musée Cernuschi: 01 53 96 21 50; 7 Av Vélasquez, 8th

RUE DES GARDES

As in the galleries of Rue Louise Weiss (see the boxed text p82), in Rue des Gardes, at the bottom of the working-class Goutte d'Or district, Paris City Council has brought together designers including **Lily Latifi** (☎ 01 42 23 30 86; www.lilylatifi.com; 11 Rue des Gardes; ⏰ 2-7pm Thu-Sat), a young Iranian designer who produces simple, evocative decorative and design objects; **Marcia de Carvalho** (☎ 01 42 51 64 05; www.marciadecarvalho .com; 2 Rue des Gardes; ⏰ 11am-7pm), with her Brazilian-inspired, feminine clothing, knits and embroidery; and the imaginative, vivid designs of Comorian designer **Sakina M'sa** (☎ 01 56 55 50 90; www.sakinamsa.com; 6 Rue des Gardes; ⏰ 10am-6pm Mon-Fri, 2-7pm Sat). See previous page for interview with Sakina M'sa.

The universe of Emmanuelle Zysman is on display in this atelier-like boutique, where his jewellery creations and bags sit alongside those of Corpus Christi, among others. Although the boutique mainly sells accessories, it also offers a small range of simply cut clothing made of high-quality materials. The brand Velvet is a particular favourite.

🏠 RUE HOUDON *Fashion*

Boutiques extend along this street. At **Séries Limitées** (number 20), you will find a wide selection of designers and a charming welcome.

The feminine creations of **Patricia Louisor** (number 16), with their distinctive coloured silk squares, are very accessible both in terms of price and wearability.

In a workshop-boutique, number 19 now houses **L'Acrobate**, a collection of children's clothes which offer an alternative to more highly coloured designs, also for

children, available from **Pamp'Lune**, 4b Rue Piémontesi, 20m further up. At number 23, rue Houdon, the designer **Tatiana Lebedev** sells a range of highly graphic clothes.

At the very end of the street, at number 5, jewellery designer **Géraldine Valluet** (who also works from this address) presents her jewellery line in a friendly atmosphere.

Most of these boutiques, as well as other shops in the district, are grouped together under the label **Les Créateurs des Abbesses** (www.les createursdesabbesses.com).

🏠 FRENCH TOUCHE
Fashion, Design

☎ 01 42 63 31 36; www.frenchtouche .com; 1 Rue Jacquemont; ⏰ 1-8pm Mon-Fri, 11am-8pm Sat; Ⓜ La Fourche
Jewellery, bags, clothing, notebooks, wallets, CDs by obscure artists, lamps, candles and charms are just a few of the items displayed on the walls or arranged on a long

table in this small boutique-gallery. French Touche offers the work of many designers, including Céline Saby (lamps) and Sandrine Colin (bags). Good range of prices.

⬛ ATELIER FRANCIADE *Crafts*
☎ 01 48 09 15 10; www.franciade.fr; 42 Rue de la Boulangerie, Saint-Denis; ⏱ noon-7pm Tue-Fri, 2-6.30pm Sat; Ⓜ Basilique de Saint-Denis

Close to the Basilique de Saint-Denis, this atelier-boutique is situated in the old crafts district. Artists and citizens draw inspiration from the archaeological finds from Saint-Denis or local heritage to make pottery, ceramics and jewellery, or else to redesign old-fashioned objects, such as stoles.

⬛ SAINT-DENIS MARKET
Fresh Produce

Place Jean-Jaurès; ⏱ 7.30am-1.30pm Tue, to 2pm Fri & Sun; Ⓜ Basilique de Saint-Denis or T1 Marché de Saint-Denis

You have to come on Sunday to get the full benefit of the atmosphere and the social interaction at this vast market (one of the largest in the Île-de-France region), part of which is sheltered by a beautiful, recently renovated hall. Like the city itself, the products on offer have a definite cosmopolitan air.

🍴 EAT

Although Montmartre is crammed with tourist traps, some of which have multilingual menus, there is no lack of more authentic eateries.

🍴 ROSE BAKERY *Tea House, Cake Shop, Delicatessen* €€
☎ 01 42 82 12 80; 46 Rue des Martyrs; ⏱ 9am-6pm Tue-Sun; Ⓜ Pigalle or Notre Dame de Lorette

There is nothing chintzy about this British-owned teashop. Quite the opposite! The stylish white space, the menu of organic salads, scones, cheesecakes and other gourmet delights represent the best the other side of the Channel has to offer. Teas,

The inviting stalls of the Saint-Denis Market

fruit juices and British fare are on sale in the grocery section.

🍴 CHEZ TOINETTE French €€
☎ 01 42 54 44 36; 20 Rue Germain-Pilon; 🕙 dinner Mon-Sat; Ⓜ Abbesses
Apart from the house speciality (duck breast with sage and honey), this bistro, which is famed for the quality of its simple dishes, also has game options (quail, doe and venison) chalked up on its blackboard.

🍴 CAFÉ BURQ
Modern Bistro €€
☎ 01 42 52 81 27; 6 Rue Burq; 🕙 from 7pm Mon-Sat; Ⓜ Abbesses
If you don't mind getting cosy with your fellow diners, this hip restaurant producing quality bistro fare (such as the classic camembert baked with honey), could be the place for you. The bar at the front fills up as the evening goes on.

🍴 LE BOUCLARD French €€€
☎ 01 45 22 60 01; 1 Rue Cavalloti; 🕙 lunch & dinner Mon-Fri, dinner only Sat; Ⓜ Place de Clichy
A restaurant to seek out on a quiet street behind the Place de Clichy, if you want to taste French cooking like grandma (well, the owner's grandma) used to make in a friendly bistro atmosphere. On the menu: braised chicken, gratin of pigs' trotters off-the-bone and an impressive côte de bœuf for two.

🍴 CHEZ SERGE French €€€
☎ 01 40 11 06 42; www.restaurant-chez-serge.com; 7 Bd Jean Jaurès, Saint-Ouen; 🕙 lunch and dinner Mon-Fri; Ⓜ Mairie de Saint-Ouen
Red and white checked tablecloths, traditional bistro cooking and the excellent wine list are to thank for the stellar success of this restaurant, which is not run by anyone called Serge, but by Caroline Montaldo.

🍴 LA FAMILLE Innovative €€€
☎ 01 42 52 11 12; 41 Rue des Trois Frères; 🕙 8pm-2am Tue-Sat; Ⓜ Abbesses
It was here that Iñaki Aizpitarte, now at Le Chateaubriand (p111), first made a splash. La Famille has not changed its credo since. The food is as deconstructed and experimental as ever. A friendly welcome.

🍸 DRINK
The neighbourhood has no shortage of charming cafés and, once again, the side streets have more to offer than the boulevards.

🍸 LA CAVE CAFÉ
Café
☎ 01 46 06 29 17; www.lacavecafe.fr; 134 Rue Marcadet; Ⓜ Lamarck Caulaincourt
This is a pleasant local bar, which is always busy and perfect for

watching the lively streets of lower Montmartre. It offers a good selection of natural wines and cocktails and there is an adjoining restaurant in case you're feeling hungry. A brunch is put on on Sundays, together with an aperitif-concert from 6.30pm.

AU RENDEZ-VOUS DES AMIS *Café, Bar*

☎ 01 46 06 01 60; www.rdvdesamis .com; 23 Rue Gabrielle; 🕙 8am-2am; Ⓜ Abbesses

Clinging to the walls of the Butte, this small bar is ideal for meeting up with friends in one of the three small rooms and avoiding the more conventional cafés of the Abbesses.

LA FOURMI *Café, Bar*

☎ 01 42 64 70 35; 74 Rue des Martyrs; 🕙 8am-2am, to 4am Fri & Sat; Ⓜ Abbesses or Pigalle

Nearly always packed, La Fourmi is conveniently located between La Cigale and Le Divan du Monde, two live-music venues. Beautiful bar and retro décor accented with modern paintings.

OLYMPIC CAFÉ *Café, Live Music Venue*

☎ 01 42 52 29 93; www.rueleon.net; 20 Rue Léon; 🕙 11am-2am Tue-Sat; Ⓜ Château Rouge

More than just a café, the Olympic is a place to meet and be entertained

(basement venue), a highlight of La Goutte d'Or. The café itself is vast and airy with 1930s tiling.

ICE KUBE *Bar*

☎ 01 42 05 20 00; www.kubehotel.com; 1-5 Passage Ruelle; 🕙 7pm-1.30am Wed-Sat, 2-11pm Sun; Ⓜ La Chapelle

Do you fancy a drink below 5°C ? If so, head to the ice bar in this high-tech building. All you have to do is make a booking and pay the fee (€38). Then you can drink four vodka-based cocktails during your allotted half-hour. Thermal suits are available. In the same building, you will find the glamorous **Bar Lounge du Kube Hotel**

Bohemian ambiance at La Fourmi

(7pm-2am) welcoming those the Ice Kube leaves cold. DJ from 8pm and brunch served on Sundays.

CAFÉ CULTUREL *Café, Live Music Venue*

☎ 01 48 20 40 62; www.cafeculturel .org; 11 Allée des Six-Chapelles, Saint-Denis; 10am-8pm Mon-Sat; M Basilique de Saint-Denis

The perfect place to sip a mint tea during the day or enjoy an evening drink. Exhibitions, concerts, storytelling and slam – the slammer Grand Corps Malade dropped his first bombs here. This café accommodating special-interest groups is a breeding ground of creativity.

PLAY

LE DIVAN DU MONDE

Live Music Venue, Club

☎ 01 40 05 06 99; www.myspace.com/ divandumonde; 75 Rue des Martyrs; entry free-€20; concerts from 7pm Thu-Sat, club 11pm-6am; M Pigalle

Le Divan has begun a new life under the artistic management of Jullian Ficarelli. The décor of this former theatre is more like an invitation to travel, with a multicultural atmosphere reflecting Africa, Europe and Asia. Live music (generally rock-electro-pop, then makes way for clubbing evenings, such as the Pigalle Rock Party.

L'ÉLYSÉE-MONTMARTRE

Live Music Venue, Club

☎ 01 44 92 45 36; www.elysee montmartre.com; 72 blvd de Rochechouart; tickets from €10; club from 11.30pm Fri & Sat; M Anvers

This lovely old room (with metalwork designed by Gustave Eiffel) hosts a diverse range of events. This is the place to come for anything from hoe down (www .myspace.com/lebal) to electro (Panik nights), disco, and punk, via gay and student nights, without forgetting the concerts, ranging from rock to hip-hop.

CHEZ MOUNE *Club*

☎ 01 45 26 64 64; 54 Rue Jean Baptiste, Pigalle; 11pm-6am Tue-Sat; M Pigalle

Recently taken over by the team from Le Baron, this former lesbian nightclub is now the in-place of lower Montmartre. With its eclectic yet carefully chosen music, a young (and mixed) crowd have made it their new place-to-be. Just remember one thing – look trendy!

LES TROIS BAUDETS

Concerts, Chansons

☎ 01 42 62 33 33; www.lestroisbaudets .com; 64 blvd de Clichy; €5-15; 6.30pm-1.30am Tue-Sat, 10am-5pm Sun; M Blanche

This old musical breeding ground from the '40s to the '60s has been

A breeding ground for young talent: the Centre Musical Fleury Goutte d'Or Barbara

revamped, although it still serves the same purpose, namely as a venue devoted to new French *chansons* (songs), with poetry and slam evenings. The line-up is packed. Two bars (6pm to 1.30am Tuesday to Saturday) and a restaurant (7pm to 12.30am Tuesday to Saturday) invite you to make in evening of it. They also put on a concert for younger audiences on Sundays at 3pm.

⭐ MAINS D'ŒUVRES
Live Music Venue

☎ 01 40 11 25 25; www.mainsdoeuvres .org; 1 Rue Charles Garnier, Saint-Ouen; entry free-€15; M Porte de Clignancourt
New music, visual arts and dance are all part of the program at this venue, managed by the same team as at Le Point Éphémère (p61).

⭐ CENTRE MUSICAL FLEURY GOUTTE D'OR BARBARA
Concerts

☎ 01 53 09 30 70; www.fgo-barbara.fr; 1 Rue de Fleury; €0-10; 11am-8pm Tue-Sat, except for concerts, up to 7pm Sun; M Barbès Rochechouart or RER B/D/E Gare du Nord
This is a place for modern-day music that welcomes curious audiences and supports young musicians. Open-stage evenings, progressive rock and electro programs are put on in a 300-seat room. Attractive contemporary architecture. For on site food and drink, head for Le Scopitone (11am to 6pm Tuesday to Friday) or Le Mange-disques (from 8pm on concert evenings).

LA VILLETTE, PANTIN, AUBERVILLIERS AND BOBIGNY: BURSTING WITH CULTURE

La Villette and its surrounding areas have changed the geographical layout of Paris and created a new way to experience the city's culture. The Parc de la Villette is in the 19th arrondissement, sandwiched between the 18th arrondissement, Pantin, Aubervilliers and La Plaine Saint-Denis, and endows the northeast of Paris its reputation as a creative and vibrant area of the city, its formerly working-class urban landscape dotted with its artists' contemporary creative offerings. Although still chaotic at times, it is an up-and-coming district.

Various music and film festivals are held in the park. Don't miss the open-air summer film festival showing mainstream and independent films, which doubles as one huge picnic. The park is basically a scaled-down version of La Villette: a spot where relaxation, leisure, culture and entertainment converge.

Finally, a few landmarks to help you get your bearings: the Grande Halle and the Cité de la Musique are on the park's south side, close to the Porte de Pantin metro station. The Cité des Sciences et de l'Industrie is to the north, close to the Porte de la Villette. The Canal de l'Ourcq runs through the centre of the park. Now it's time to see it for yourself!

LA VILLETTE, PANTIN, AUBERVILLIERS AND BOBIGNY

See map on following pages

One of the geometrically designed follies (architect Bernard Tschumi) scattered across the Parc de la Villette,

◎ SEE

The Parc de la Vilette, the largest green space in Paris, is home to a number of cultural centres located in its grounds.

◎ PARC DE LA VILLETTE

☎ 01 40 03 75 75; www.villette.com; 211 Av Jean Jaurès; Ⓜ Porte de Pantin

An innovation in more than one sense, this park has no fences. A space that is open to the city, where architecture and landscape fuse together, this city park was designed by the Swiss-French architect Bernard Tschumi. Its layout includes points (the 'follies' – the strange red structures that are dotted around the park), lines (paths – the Galerie de la Villette and Galerie de l'Ourcq) and spaces (areas of grass and gardens). The park, which at first glance appears visually fragmented, is in fact highly structured in a similar way to an abstract work of art. Thousands of discoveries are waiting to be made as you stroll along its paths.

From spring onwards, the grass is packed with families or people just there to chill out. The drumbeats of *djembe* (skin-covered hand drum shaped like a large goblet) players echo through the park, people can be seen honing their *capoeira* skills, and *batacudas* (Brazilian percussion instruments) enter the mix on Saturday or Sunday mornings when there are rehearsals.

◎ LA GRANDE HALLE

Ⓜ Porte de Pantin

A typical example of industrial architecture, this former cattle market has kept its clock from the days of the Paris abattoirs.

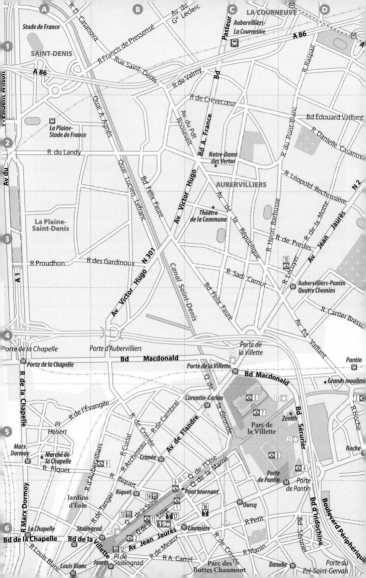

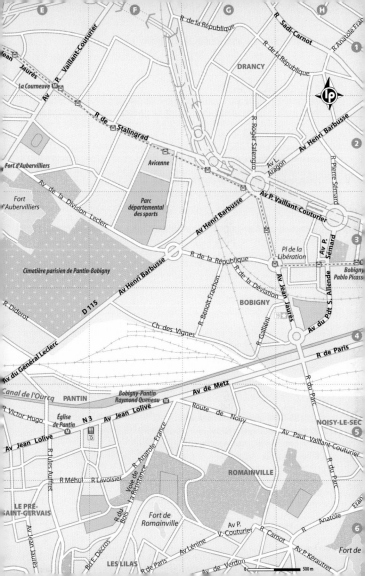

THE CANAL BY BOAT

Why not take a cruise to discover the neighbourhood? Be warned, however, that part of the trip along the Canal Saint-Martin takes place underground (after the Faubourg du Temple). Also steer clear if you are impatient as the lock gates slow things down considerably, spinning the trip out to two hours 30 minutes.

Canauxrama (☎ 01 42 39 15 00; www.canauxrama.com; 13 Quai de la Loire; adults/students/senior citizens or children/under 4 yrs €15/11/8/free, single rate on the weekend, afternoons & public holidays; ☯ 9.45am & 2.45pm from Apr-Oct). Leaving from the Bassin de la Villette, Canauxrama's boats reach the port at the Arsenal, close to the Bastille, via the Canal Saint-Martin. Canauxrama also organises trips along the Canal Saint-Denis.

Paris Canal (☎ 01 42 40 96 97; www.pariscanal.com; 21 Quai de la Loire; adults/12-15 yrs/senior citizens or 4-11 yrs €17/14/10; ☯ end Mar–mid-Nov) Scheduled trips as far as the Musée d'Orsay (part of the journey is along the Seine). Departures at 2.30pm from the Parc de la Villette, close to the footbridge, on the Galerie de la Villette side.

Base Nautique de la Villette (☎ 01 42 40 29 90; 41 bis Quai de la Loire; free; ☯ 9am-noon & 2-5pm every 45 mins Sat) If you fancy burning off some energy, here is your chance to discover the pleasures of rowing, canoeing and kayaking in the middle of Paris. Book a week in advance.

It was restored by the architects Reichen and Robert. This large and impressive exhibition centre and venue also has an on-site bookshop as well as a great restaurant.

◉ CITÉ DE LA MUSIQUE

☎ 01 44 84 45 00; www.cite-musique.fr; 221 Av Jean Jaurès; concerts €8-39; ☯ noon-6pm Tue-Sat, 10am-6pm Sun; Ⓜ Porte de Pantin; ♿

Apart from the numerous events on offer, the building itself is well worth a visit. Playing with shapes, perspective and light, Christian de Portzamparc has designed a city layout with roads, squares and staircases, such as the Rue de la Trompe, which winds its way in a spiral around the concert hall designed with the help of composer Pierre Boulez. The Cité de la Musique also has a multimedia library, a contemporary music archive centre and a fabulous **museum** (☎ 01 44 84 44 84; guided visit full price/concs €10/5, Sat & Sun at 3pm with prior booking, non-guided visit €8, free for under 26yrs; noon-6pm Tue-Sat, 10am-6pm Sun) that has just been revamped. It features a collection of over 900 instruments ranging from the 17th century to the present day.Two temporary exhibitions also take place every year as the *We Want Miles*. In 2012, a large auditorium designed by Jean Nouvel will be opened in the Cité, which will become home to the Philharmonie de Paris (Paris Symphony Society).

☉ CITÉ DES SCIENCES ET DE L'INDUSTRIE

☎ 01 40 05 70 00; www.cite-sciences. fr; full price/concs €3-10/€3-8 depending on the site, full price/concs passes €15.50-17.50/€14; ☽ 10am-6pm Tue-Sat, to 7pm Sun; Ⓜ Porte de la Villette; ⚒ except for the Argonaute

Learning through fun is the principle behind this enormous science museum, with its unusual attractions such as the **Cité des Enfants**, which has one space for children aged two to seven years and another for children aged five to 12 years. Other attractions include entertaining and informative exhibitions such as the interactive and educational Exploras.

The **Géode** (☎ 01 39 17 10 00; www .lageode.fr; 26 Av Courentin Cariou; full price/concs €10.50/9; ⚒), the perfectly spherical structure from which light bounces off, is without doubt the most fascinating feature of the whole park. The cinema has a giant 360-degree screen with a projection system and reclining seats, placing the viewer at the heart of the image. The Géode also stages musical events with a series

of electro-pop-rock concerts. Next to the Géode, venture inside the **Argonaute** (☽ 10.30am-5.30pm Tue-Sat, to 6.30pm Sun), a former naval submarine from the '50s where you can see everything, from the engine rooms to the crew's quarters.

☉ BASSIN DE LA VILLETTE

Quai de la Seine & Quai de la Loire;
Ⓜ **Jaurès or Stalingrad**
The Bassin de la Villette is an entirely different world. It all began a few years ago when the MK2–Quai de Seine cinema complex was built close to the Ledoux Rotunda. Parisians soon flocked to this area's

A relaxed stroll along the banks of the Bassin

LA VILLETTE, PANTIN, AUBERVILLIERS AND BOBIGNY

impressive facilities and quayside cafés. Another cinema has since been built opposite the first one, on the other side of the Bassin: the MK2–Quai de Loire boasts a café and a great bookshop (look out for the neon designs by Martial Raysse). A little ferry (€0.50; free with a cinema ticket) will take you from one side of the Bassin to the other, on what is bound to be an entertaining trip.

On the other end of the Bassin, on the Quai de Seine side, the former *Magasins Généraux* (storehouses for the capital's building materials, coal, wood…) have undergone a huge transformation while remaining in keeping with the style and size of the warehouse on the opposite bank. A youth hostel has now set up shop there, and its brightly painted bar, open to the public, provides an ideal and interesting meeting place.

Picnics, *pétanque* (the bowling game particularly popular in the south of France), jogging, bike rides and walks from Stalingrad to La Villette are the most popular activities on a sunny day. Nowadays the Bassin hosts one site of Paris Plages (the French capital's answer to beach culture) in August and Puces du Design (Design Flea Markets) in the autumn.

CENTRE NATIONAL DE LA DANSE

☎ 01 41 83 98 98; www.cnd.fr; 1 Rue Victor Hugo, Pantin; €6-18 ; ☷ 9am-7pm Mon-Fri, to 10pm on performance nights; Ⓜ Hoche or RER E Pantin; ♿

A place worth visiting as much for its architecture as for its performances, this is a showcase for contemporary dance and a hotbed of young talent. Exposed concrete takes pride of place here, as demonstrated by the impressive central staircase known as the *'rampe cyclopéenne'* (Cyclopean ramp). A magnificent sight when it is illuminated at night, the CND also looks pretty good by day. You can dine in the café-restaurant with a terrace overlooking the Canal de l'Ourcq.

The Cité de la Musique (p134) and its café

THE CANAL SAINT-DENIS BY BIKE

Here are two suggested itineraries for cycling from La Villette to Pantin or Saint-Denis. You can also use the public bicycle-hire system Vélib' (p159).

La Villette–Pantin: Cycle along the Bassin de la Villette (p135) before reaching the Canal de l'Ourcq where it intersects with the Canal Saint-Denis. Cross the park, then pass under the bridge carrying the Périphérique (city ring road), remaining on the cycle path alongside the canal (it bears slightly left). You will now be near the old windmills in Pantin, currently in the process of being restored. In Pantin you can use the footbridges either to cross to the opposite bank or to get back to the town.

La Villette–Aubervilliers–Saint-Denis: Leave the Parc de la Villette from the north side. Dismount to take the Quai de la Charente (a one-way street) and then go down the Quai de l'Allier, on the right bank of the canal. In no time, you will be out of Paris and inside Aubervilliers, close to the first locks. The canal is still in use and barges arrive to load up at the warehouses. You will first go past the Parc de l'Ecluse (in the Pont-Tournant district), the first of the gardens that are strung along the canal. Further on, you'll see the Passerelle de la Fraternité footbridge built in honour of the Algerians who died in the Parisian massacre of October 1961. You'll catch a glimpse of the lovely Élie-Lotar park to one side. To get to the Stade de France (stadium), leave the canal side at the Franc-Moisin swing-bridge and follow Rue Delaunay.

☾ LE CENTQUATRE

☎ 01 53 35 50 00; www.104.fr; 104 Rue d'Aubervilliers or 5 rue Curial; free entry; ☽ 11am-8pm Tue-Thu & Sun, 11am-11pm Fri & Sat; Ⓜ Stalingrad or Crimée

Housed in the former city funeral parlour, this hive of artistic activity was opened in 2008 and has 15 teams of artists in residency from all over the world, involved in a variety of fields (fashion, design, visual arts, fine art and digital art). The workshops are open two weekends per month to encourage exchanges with the public. Other events and guided visits (that may be of interest to children) are available. Works of art can be viewed free of charge in the passage. This site also has a restaurant, a very hip pizza van and an attractive café. An Emmaüs charity shop (3pm to 6pm Wednesday to Saturday) – the first of its kind in this part of Paris – now attracts middle-class bohemians from the surrounding areas.

☾ LES LABORATOIRES D'AUBERVILLIERS

☎ 01 53 56 15 90; www.leslaboratoires .org; 41 Rue Lécuyer, Aubervilliers; entry free–€5; Ⓜ Aubervilliers-Pantin Quatre Chemins

This venue was conceived by the Aubervilliers Town Council and

NEIGHBOURHOODS

LA VILLETTE, PANTIN, AUBERVILLIERS AND BOBIGNY

initially run by the choreographer François Verret. Housed in a former factory measuring 900 sq metres, the Laboratoires focus on artistic research – various projects are run simultaneously – and aim to forge relationships between different disciplines. Performances, exhibitions and films are regularly put on for the public (you can find the programme on the website).

🍴 EAT

La Villette has fast-food stands and a fairground stall selling treats for those with a sweet tooth, right next to the merry-go-rounds and the Canal de l'Ourcq, or you can always go for the option of picnicking on the grass. There are also some great little eateries close by.

🍴 LE BASTRINGUE
Bistro　€
☎ 01 42 09 89 27; 67 Quai de la Seine; 🕐 9am-2am Mon-Fri, 5pm-2am Sat; Ⓜ Riquet
The dark-pink façade hides a great traditional bar where locals from the area mix with a young arty crowd. In addition, the location – just in front of the Bassin de la Villette – is quite something. It is packed at lunchtime and with good reason – the pies and salads are delicious. The menu gains a bit more substance in the evening (scallops flambéed in brandy or beef tenderloin) and the atmosphere

becomes livelier, helped along by shots of infused rum.

🍴 CÔTÉ CANAL
Café, Restaurant　€
☎ 01 40 36 92 49; www.cotecanal.fr; 5 Quai de la Seine; 🕐 10am-1am; Ⓜ Jaurès or Stalingrad
Enjoy the down-to-earth, sociable atmosphere in this café-restaurant. Portions are generous and consist of classic dishes such as tournedos steak, leg of lamb and Morteau sausage – hearty stuff! However, those with smaller appetites can order a salad. Art is exhibited on the walls, occasional poetry readings are organised and there are gigs on the weekend if the weather is good.

🍴 25ᵉ EST *Bar-Restaurant*　€
☎ 01 42 09 66 74; www.25est.com; 10 Place de la Bataille de Stalingrad; 🕐 11am-2am Tue-Sat; Ⓜ Jaurès or Stalingrad
Point your compass 25 degrees east: 25ᵉ Est is next to Bassin de la Villette, behind Ledoux Rotunda. Dishes are simple and pleasingly modern (terrine of aubergine and salmon, duck breast with honey and balsamic vinegar, salmon à la plancha). In summer, its two-level terrace a few steps from the water's edge is a must for chilling out. Inside, basic décor brings to mind trendy venues in Berlin. The bar holds events, debates, exhibitions and gigs of all kinds.

🍴 CAFÉ DE LA MUSIQUE
Brasserie €€
☎ 01 48 03 15 91; Place de la Fontaine aux Lions, 213 Av Jean Jaurès;
🕐 9am-1am Sun-Thu, to 2am Fri & Sat;
Ⓜ Porte de Pantin

Worth a visit for the terrace alone! Sleekly designed inside, its atmosphere is cosily fashionable. Perfect for private conversations. The menu combines contemporary dishes with traditional fare (avocado and prawn mousse and grilled tuna steak). Sunday brunch is available (noon to 4pm).

🍴 LE PLATE'S
French €€€
☎ 01 57 42 93 14; www.leplates.fr; 140 Av Jean Lolive, Pantin;
🕐 lunch Mon-Fri, dinner Wed-Sat;
Ⓜ Église de Pantin

A fasionable spot in Pantin, Le Plate's offers a substantial menu with original dishes such as fillet of duck breast on stewed pineapple with a hint of black pepper. A large restaurant with a simple modernist design, brightened up by the garden it overlooks.

🍸 DRINK

It's hard to find more attractive terraces in Paris than those along the canal from the Bassin de la Villette. On fine days, ever-changing groups form and dissolve, taking turns to linger at the water's edge, drinks in hand.

Bar Ourq (p140) is a pleasant spot to have a drink

BAR OURCQ *Bar*

☎ 01 42 40 12 26; 68 Quai de la Loire; 3pm-midnight Wed-Thu, 3pm-2am Fri & Sat, 3-10pm Sun; M Laumière
This is a truly eye-catching building with its turquoise façade. Young good-looking trendy types with alternative leanings come here to relax. Live music and DJs at the weekends and on the evenings before public holidays. There are board games, *pétanque*, wi-fi access on offer. A few deckchairs are on the terrace next to the canal.

ABRACADABAR *Café, Live Music Venue*

www.abracadabar.fr; 123 Av Jean Jaurès; from 6pm; M Laumière or Ourcq
Don't be fooled by its deserted-looking appearance. Though it is located on a fairly unprepossessing street, this café-gig venue is a welcome oasis. It mostly gets crowded for gigs starting at 8.30pm or 9pm and for DJ nights starting at 11pm. Check out the website for the latest programme.

PLAY

CABARET SAUVAGE *Concerts, Club*

☎ 01 42 09 01 09; www.cabaretsauvage.com; Parc de la Villette, pedestrian access via 59 blvd Mac Donald; tickets €18-25; M Porte de la Villette
It's difficult not to fall under the spell of this venue at the edge

Boogie the night away at the Cabaret Sauvage!

of the Canal de l'Ourcq, situated inside an enormous brightly coloured tent with wooden beams and red velvet awning. The varied programme includes parties and dances, spellbinding musical performances and fun cabaret shows. Goran Bregovic, PJ Harvey, Yuri Buenaventura, Los Van Van and even Raul Paz are among those to have performed at the Cabaret! In winter, the *Folles Nuits Berbères* shows are a real treat (for tastebuds too, with a selection of Berber dishes) as are *Les Nuits Gypsy du Vrai-Faux Mariage*.

⭐ TRABENDO *Concerts*
☎ 01 49 25 89 99; www.trabendo.fr; Parc de La Villette; Porte de Pantin, Ⓜ Porte de La Villette

The Trabendo is located in one of the red 'follies' (see p131) of the Parc de la Villette. Designer Kristian Gavoille has revamped the interior, now decorated with murals by American graffiti artist Futura 2000. Careful programming, combining tenors from the electro scene, bands such as Calexico and Supergrass and festivals of modern music.

⭐ GLAZ'ART
Live Music Venue, Club
☎ 01 40 36 55 65; www.glazart. com; 7-15 Av de la Porte de la Villette; €8-15; Ⓜ Porte de la Villette

Located near the Paris city gates, in a kind of no-man's land, Glaz'art is a spot for night owls. An old bus station has been converted into a friendly venue with a colourful décor bordering on kitsch. On offer: gigs and underground DJs (post-rock, punk, baroque, electro, hip hop…), eclectic nights, dances with accordion music, projections and exhibitions by resident artists. In the summer, from June to September, *La Plage* (free entry; 7pm to midnight Wednesday to Saturday), with its garden and straw hut, is the ideal place to take some fresh air.

⭐ CANAL 93 *Concerts*
☎ information 01 49 91 10 50, tickets 01 48 30 83 29; www.canal 93.net; 63 Av Jean Jaurès, Bobigny; entry free-€15; Ⓜ Pablo Picasso then bus 301, stop Louise Michel, or T1 Libération

A venue dedicated to the latest music, Canal 93 holds around 40 concerts a year, including hip-hop, slam, funk and jazz. The monthly open jam session is a huge success. There is a free shuttle to Porte de Pantin on certain nights. Once there, the Restaurant 63 offers good at low prices, with a €20 dinner-show.

PARIS

Paris isn't the only place to find centres of creativity and promotion of the arts. There are a number of contemporary art hotspots surrounding the capital. Often offering the unexpected, such as the Cyclop, the Villa Savoye or the Dubuffet Foundation, they are generally accessible by public transport.

The Domaine Départemental de Chamarande (p148)

THE NORTH AND EAST

ABBAYE DE MAUBUISSON

Saint-Ouen-l'Aumône

☎ 01 34 64 36 10; Rue Richard de Tour; abbey full price/concs/under 25yrs €3.80/3/free; ✆ abbey 1-6pm Wed-Mon, 2-6pm Sat & Sun, grounds 8am-6.30pm daily mid-Sep–mid-Mar, 7am-9pm daily mid-Mar–mid-Sep; Ⓜ RER C towards Pontoise to Saint-Ouen-l'Aumône

Here, contemporary art is set against a Cistercian backdrop. A number of light and airy rooms remain of the Abbey founded in 1236 by the mother of King Saint Louis, Blanche de Castille,

which have been converted into exhibition spaces. Solo and collective exhibitions are also held in the barn and the grounds. The work of both established (Orlan, Erik Samakh, Olga Kisseleva, François Daireaux) and emerging artists is showcased here in installations that are often designed for the Abbey. The pretty tree-lined park, with its stream, canal and mirror lakes spread over an eight-hectare expanse, is an ideal spot to settle down for a picnic.

You can grab a bite to eat three minutes' walk from the Abbey at: **Le Petit Gris** (☎ 01 34 64 90 89; 2 Rue Jean-Jaurès; ✆ Sat). The set menu on offer will cost you approximately €15. It is essential that you make reservations in order to dine here.

CENTRE D'ART CONTEMPORAIN DE LA FERME DU BUISSON

Noisiel/Marne-la-Vallée

☎ 01 64 62 77 77; www.laferme dubuisson.com; Allée de la Ferme, Noisiel; full price/concs €2/1; ✆ centre 2-8pm Wed, Sat & Sun; Ⓜ RER A towards Marne-la-Vallée–Chessy to Noisiel–Le Luzard

La Ferme du Buisson is a cultural polyglot, offering dance, theatre, cinema, live music, and more. Situated in one of the wings of this abandoned 19th-century industrial site, the Centre d'Art Contemporain

Abbaye de Maubuisson

features an interesting programme that favours an approach that is both forward-looking (with young artists or artists rarely shown in France) and multidisciplinary (the artistic offerings often bring together a number of art forms, as in the recent 'choreographed exhibition').

There is a restaurant in the grounds of La Ferme: the **Relais du Buisson** (☎ 01 60 17 17 25; www.lerelais dubuisson.com; ☽ lunch Sun-Fri, dinner Tue-Sat).

CENTRE PHOTOGRAPHIQUE D'ÎLE-DE-FRANCE
Pontault-Combault

☎ 01 70 05 49 80; www.cpif.net; 107 Av de la République; free entry; ☽ 10am-6pm Wed-Fri, 2-6pm Sat & Sun, guided tour 3pm Sun; Ⓜ RER E towards Tournan to Émerainville-Pontault-Combault

This centre focuses on photography, as well as art forms associated with still and moving images. It is notable for its eclecticism, with exhibitions sometimes entrusted to foreign curators, and its willingness to engage with the public. Opportunities to meet with the artists are therefore frequently arranged.

Pontault-Combault is home to a large Portuguese community, so a visit to the Centre Photographique d'Île-de-France is an ideal chance to

sample their cuisine. Good choices nearby include: **Chez Carlos** (☎ 01 60 29 63 84; 93 Av de la République), a 10-seat restaurant noted for its *churrasco* (rôtisserie), and the larger **Iha Doce** (☎ 01 60 29 21 01; 72 Av Charles-Rouxel), which offers set menus from €10 to €18.

LA GALERIE, CENTRE D'ART CONTEMPORAIN
Noisy-le-Sec

☎ 01 49 42 67 17; www.dca-art.com; 1 Rue Jean Jaurès; free entry; ☽ 2-6pm Tue-Fri, to 7pm Sat; Ⓜ Mairie des Lilas then bus 105 to Jeanne d'Arc; or Ⓜ Église de Pantin then bus 145 to Jeanne d'Arc; or RER E towards Chelles-Tournan to Noisy-le-Sec; or T1 terminus

Little-known works are often displayed at the Galerie, which each year welcomes a resident plastic artist and a foreign curator. The painter Adam Adach chose this as the venue for his first solo exhibition in the Île-de-France region. Four exhibitions are held each year, displaying new works by internationally renowned artists, as well as emerging names.

While visiting the Galerie, why not take the opportunity to explore the **Cité Expérimentale du Merlan**? This was constructed after WWII in order to rehouse residents of the badly bombed town. A total of 43 houses line the streets off Av du Général Leclerc.

MUSÉE DE L'AIR
ET DE L'ESPACE *Le Bourget*
☎ 01 49 92 70 00; www.mae.org;
Aéroport de Paris, Le Bourget;
permanent collection free entry,
aeroplanes full price/concs €6/4,
planetarium €5/3, guided tour €10/7.50;
🕙 10am-6pm Tue-Sun Apr-Sep, to 5pm
Oct-Mar; Ⓜ La Courneuve then bus 152;
or RER B towards Aéroport CDG-Mitry-
Claye to Le Bourget then bus 152

Established in 1915, the airport was
converted into a museum in 1973,
when the Aéroport de Roissy was
opened. From the pioneers behind
Concorde (which you can visit) and
the Boeing 747, to military aircraft
and space travel, illustrated by
models of the Ariane 1 and 5 rockets
and the planetarium, the museum
is a must for all those people
fascinated by flying machines. As
well as exploring a cockpit and
trying out the flight simulator (€10
and €5, only available during the
school holidays), children visiting
the brand new Planète Pilote area
can learn about air and space
through an interactive 1½-hour visit
that features lots of fun experiments.

THE SOUTH
CATHÉDRALE DE
LA RÉSURRECTION *Évry*
☎ 01 64 97 93 53; www.cathedrale-evry
.cef.fr/sansfenetre; Cours Monseigneur-
Roméro; free entry; 🕙 10am-noon &

The tree-lined roof of the Cathédrale in Évry

2-6pm Mon-Sat, 2.30-7pm Sun; Ⓜ RER
D towards Malesherbes to Évry-
Courcouronnes

The Swiss architect Mario Botta is to
thank for this stunning cathedral in
the heart of the new town of Évry,
which opened its doors in 1995.
Designed as a 'house consisting
of a single floor, stretching from
the heavens to earth', this circular
building (which looks like a
truncated cylinder from the outside)
is made of more than 800,000 bricks
(crafted in Toulouse) arranged to
form a geometrical design. The
roof is crowned with lime trees,
symbolising life.

Within the building, the new
Musée Paul-Delouvrier (☎ 01 60 75
02 71; www.museepauldelouvrier.com;

12 Clos de la Cathédrale, Évry) boasts a contemporary art department.

In summer, the terrace of a nearby Indian and Nepalese restaurant, **Le Chemin d'Himalaya** (☎ 01 60 77 87 45; www.chemindehimalaya.fr; 12-14 Cours Monseigneur Roméro) offers views of the exterior.

DOMAINE DÉPARTEMENTAL DE CHAMARANDE *Chamarande*
☎ 01 60 82 52 01; www.chamarande. essonne.fr; 38 Rue du Commandant Arnoux; free entry; ⏱ grounds 9am-6pm Oct, Feb & Mar, to 5pm Nov-Jan & Apr-May, to 8pm Jun-Sep, Château and

The work of Peter Coffin, Domaine de Chamarande

Orangerie depending on exhibitions; Ⓜ RER C towards St-Martin-d'Étampes to Chamarande

The Domaine Départemental de Chamarande consists of a 17th-century château and *orangerie*, hosting contemporary art exhibitions which aim to interact with the rich heritage of the surroundings. It also has beautiful landscaped grounds (98 hectare), dotted with surprising and evocative sculptures, including specially commissioned works by Gloria Friedmann and Philippe Ramette. A programme of summer events is held in the grounds (including dance and cinema).

Follow your visit with a stroll in the Forêt du Belvédère, to the north of the village of Chamarande, which gives an unobstructed view of the Domaine. It is also a perfect place to enjoy a picnic.

DUBUFFET FOUNDATION
Périgny-sur-Yerres
☎ 01 47 34 12 63; www.dubuffet fondation.com/actuset.htm; Rue du Moulin Neuf; full price/concs €8/4.50; ⏱ year-round except Mon, Wed & public holidays, by arrangement only; Ⓜ RER A Boissy-Saint-Léger then bus 4023

The Dubuffet Foundation is worth the detour for the awe-inspiring Closerie Falbala, a giant sculpture (and listed historic monument) measuring 1610 sq metres. At its heart is the Villa Falbala, which was

SOUND OF THE SUBURBS

A number of venues with exciting live listings are worth making the trip out of the city. For example: **Le Plan** (☎ 01 69 02 09 19; www.leplan.com) in Ris-Orangis, is a seminal rock venue that hosts superb, of-the-moment gigs; the **Emb** (☎ 01 39 80 01 39; www.emb-sannois.org) in Sannois stands out with its eclectic, audacious and always excellent line-ups (Izabo, Sharko and Tiken Jah Fakoly, among others), and the **Usine à Chapeaux** (☎ 01 30 88 89 04; www .mjc-rambouillet.asso.fr) in Rambouillet is a hub of musical activism (Winston McAnuff, Beat Assailant, Electro Deluxe…) and breeding ground for new talent.

constructed to house the Cabinet Logologique (a philosophical chamber designed by and for Dubuffet as a total retreat from day-to-day life). An adjoining building also displays the *Practicables* and *Costumes* of Dubuffet's animated painting *Coucou Bazar*, as well as some of his paintings.

LE CYCLOP *Milly-la-Forêt*
☎ 01 64 98 83 17; www.lecyclop.com; **Bois des Pauvres; guided tour full price/ concs €7/6, under 8yrs not admitted;** guided tours every 45 min 2-5pm Sat, 11am-5.45pm Sun May-Oct
The huge Cyclops-headed totem by Swiss sculptor Jean Tinguely towers in the heart of the Milly forest. The 300 tonnes of steel used to create the 22m-high structure form an enchanting world. Visitors are invited to venture inside this giant and discover works by a handful of artists Tinguely involved in his adventure, including Niki de Saint Phalle, Jean-Pierre Raynaud, César, Jesus Raphael Soto and Éva Aeppli.

Apart from the Milly forest, the Trois Pignons and Fontainebleau forests offer charming walks in the surrounding area. All three are popular tracks with hikers and climbers.

To get there, take highway A6 exit 13 Milly-la-Forêt, towards Milly. At Milly head towards Étampes (D837) then take the road to the right after 200m.

THE WEST
ACADÉMIE DU SPECTACLE ÉQUESTRE *Versailles*
☎ 0892 68 18 91; www.acadequestre.fr; **Grande Ecurie du château, Av Rockefeller;** *Matinales des Écuyers* **€12, Academy visit €6/5, combined** *Matinales* **& château ticket €21;** 11.15am Sat & Sun; **M** RER C Versailles–Rive-Gauche
A different way to discover the Château de Versailles is to visit the Grande Écurie Royale stables or, even better, see one of the *Matinales des Écuyers* (morning dressage sessions) of the Académie Équestre

Fireworks light up the Bassin of the Château de Versailles

that is run by Bartabas, where you get to see the riders who work on the art of dressage every day, practising with their magnificent horses. In the background, Baroque music alternates with the voices of great equerries speaking about their art. Shows take place in the evening.

The living heart of Versailles beats at La Place du Marché Notre-Dame, where you will find numerous restaurants on the square itself and in the surrounding streets, including **Sister's Café** (☎ 01 30 21 21 22; 15 Rue des Réservoirs) which cooks up a mean burger and weekend brunch, and **Le Cameleone Café** (☎ 01 30 21 90 90; 19 Rue Pourvoierie) with its unbeatable steak tartare.

FÊTES DE VERSAILLES AND VERSAILLES OFF *Versailles*

☎ 01 30 83 78 89; www.chateauversailles-spectacles.fr; Fêtes de Versailles seats €35-85, Versailles Off €13.50; ⏲ Fêtes de Versailles summer evenings, Versailles Off every autumn, during Château opening hours & to 10pm Sat; Ⓜ RER C Versailles–Rive Gauche; or bus 171 to Versailles–Place d'Armes

Like the Académie du Spectacle Équestre (p149), the Fêtes de Versailles are another alternative way to explore Versailles. Held from June to September at the Bassin de Neptune in the Château grounds, spectacular displays (equestrian, aquatic, pyrotechnic) are staged by artists from all disciplines (including dance and theatre) who revive the spirit of the celebrations of the *Grand Siècle* under Louis XIV. Every year, the Château also showcases the work of a major contemporary artist in the royal apartments and around the gardens, creating ties between Versailles and the art of today. Recent cycles were inaugurated in 2008 by Jeff Koons, followed by Xavier Veilhan the following year and Takashi Murakami in 2010.

CENTRE NATIONAL DE L'ESTAMPE ET DE L'ART IMPRIMÉ *Chatou*

☎ 01 39 52 45 35; www.cneai.com; 2 Rue du Bac; Île des Impressionnistes; free entry; 🕑 noon-6pm Tue-Sun; Ⓜ RER A towards Saint-Germain-en-Laye to Rueil-Malmaison then N190 towards Chatou

Don't be deceived by the somewhat institutional title given to this National Centre of Etchings and Printed Art, perched on the Île des Impressionnistes, a favourite haunt of the fauvists and Impressionists. More than just a gallery, the CNEAI is devoted to the publication of its artists and each year opens its doors to around 10 artists in residence. A collection of 300 pieces has been built up in this way, added to which are more than 9000 *ephemeras* (stickers, posters,

artist reviews, records, newspapers and postcards) demonstrating different processes (digital printing, offset, etching, photocopying…). The Bouroullec brothers created a 'floating house' for the centre, a houseboat dedicated to artists' projects.

Elsewhere on the island, the **Musée Fournaise** (☎ 01 34 80 63 22; www.musee-fournaise.com) has a collection of Impressionist and fauvist works, and two restaurants.

VILLA SAVOYE *Poissy*

☎ 01 39 65 01 06; www.villa-savoye.monuments-nationaux.fr; 82 Rue de Villiers; guided tour full price/concs/under 18yrs €7/4.50/free; 🕑 10am-5pm Mar-Apr, Sep & Oct, to 6pm May-August, to 1pm Nov-Feb Tue-Sun; Ⓜ RER A Poissy, then bus 50 towards La Coudraie to Villa-Savoye or Lycée-Le-Corbusier

This villa, which was constructed by Le Corbusier between 1928 and 1931, is a perfect example of the architect's style. The clean lines of the white, parallel-piped building are supported by narrow stilts and topped with a roof terrace. The play of light enlivens the building, which, to use Le Corbusier's words, makes this villa not just a *'machine à habiter'*, but also a *'machine à émouvoir'*, a moving work of art as well as a structure to inhabit.

DIRECTORY
PRACTICALITIES

TOURIST INFORMATION

Tourist information points offer travellers practical and cultural information, ticket sales and tourist passes (Paris Museum Pass, public transport, concerts, museums, exhibitions, hotel reservations, dinner cruises, city tours, etc.). They are located in airport terminals at Roissy Charles de Gaulle, Orly Sud and in Versailles:

Roissy-Charles de Gaulle Airport
Terminal 1 (Arrivals, gate 4; ☺ 7am-8.30pm); Terminal 2C (Arrivals/departures, opposite gate 5; ☺ 7am-2.15pm); Terminal 2D (Arrivals/departures, gate 5; ☺ 8am-10.30pm); Terminal 2E (Arrivals, level 0, E/F connecting walkway; ☺ 7am-9.30pm); Terminal 2F (Arrivals, level 0, gate 11; ☺ 7am-9.30pm)

Orly Sud Airport (Arrivals, gate L; ☺ 7.15am-9.30pm)

Versailles Tourist Office (2 bis Av de Paris; ☺ 10am-6pm Mon, 9am-7pm Tue-Sun)

Disneyland Resort Paris (opposite the Disney Village entrance; ☺ 9am-8.45pm)

Paris Tourist Office (www.parisinfo.com; 25-27 Rue des Pyramides, 1st; ☺ 10am-7pm Mon-Sat, 11am-7pm Sun & public holidays; Ⓜ Pyramides) It also operates other centres in Paris (Anvers, Gare du Nord, Gare de Lyon and Gare de l'Est, Paris Expo-Porte de Versailles and the Montmartre Tourist Information Office).

ACCOMMODATION

From sumptuous palaces to modest neighbourhood hotels, Paris has no fewer than 1500 places to stay. Useful links for room bookings:

Accor (www.accorhotels.com)
Adagio City Hôtels (www.adagio-city.com)
Alcôves & Agapes (www.bed-and-breakfast-in-paris.com)
Exclusive Hôtels (www.exclusive-hotels.fr)
Home Plazza (www.homeplazza.com)
Hôtels de Paris (www.hotels-paris.com)
Intervac (www.intervac.fr) Home exchange
Meeting the French (www.meetingthefrench.com) Selection of B&B rooms

BUSINESS HOURS

Shops and offices are usually closed on Sundays and sometimes on Mondays (particularly banks). Some shops stay open until 10pm one day a week (usually Thursday). Banks are open from 9am to 4pm, but some close at lunchtime.

Restaurants are generally open for lunch from 12pm to 3pm and from 7pm or 7.30pm until at least 9.30pm for dinner. The ticket kiosks for monuments and museums close half an hour to an hour before the sites.

DISCOUNTS

A large number of discounts (between 30% and 50%) are granted to young people, students and pensioners for all kinds of services from public transport to museums. Don't forget your ID and flash it at every opportunity.

GUIDED TOURS

BY BUS

A few companies offer excursions and guided tours in central Paris and the surrounding area by coach or minibus.

Cityrama (☎ 01 44 55 60 00; www.paris cityrama.com; 149 Rue Saint-Honoré, 1st; Ⓜ Pyramides or Opéra)

Les Cars Rouges (☎ 01 53 953 953; www.carsrouges.com; 17 Quai de Grenelle, 15th; ticket €24/12). Tour lasts two hours 15 minutes. Ticket valid for two consecutive days. Various stops: Eiffel Tower, Musée du Louvre, Musée d'Orsay, Opéra–Galeries Lafayette, Champs-Élysées–Étoile, Grand Palais…

Paris Vision (☎ 01 42 60 30 01; www.parisvision.com; 214 Rue de Rivoli, 1st; Ⓜ Tuileries)

France Tourisme (☎ 01 53 10 35 35; www.francetourisme.fr; 33 Quai des Grands-Augustins, 6th; Ⓜ Saint-Michel)

Paris l'Open Tour (☎ 01 42 66 56 56; www.parislopentour.com; 13 Rue Auber, 9th; 1-day ticket €29/15; Ⓜ Havre-Caumartin or Opéra) Four routes with commentaries in several languages aboard a double-decker bus. Paris Grand Tour: duration two hours 15 minutes.

BY BOAT

A number of companies run tours along the Seine and its charming canals.

Canal cruises

See the boxed text on p134 for details.

Cruises along the Seine

Bateaux Parisiens (☎ 0825 01 01 01; www.bateauxparisiens.com; Port de la Bourdonnais, 7th; tickets €11/5; ☒ every 30 min 10am-10.30pm Apr-Sep, every hour 10am-10pm Oct-Mar; Ⓜ Alma Marceau). Hour-long tours with commentaries in 13 languages. Departures from the foot of the Eiffel Tower. There are also several daily departures from Notre-Dame (€12/6). **Vedettes de Paris** (☎ 01 44 18 19 50; www.vedettesdeparis. fr; Port de Suffren, 7th; tickets €11/5; ☒ every 30 min 11am-9pm Mar-Apr & Sep, 10.30am-11pm Jul-Aug, every hour 11am-6pm Jan, Feb & Oct-Dec; Ⓜ Bir Hakeim). Hour long open-topped cruise in several languages. Departures from the foot of the Eiffel Tower.

ON FOOT

Ça Se Visite! (☎ 01 43 57 59 50; www.ca-se-visite.fr; walking tour €10/12) Parisians lead small groups on guided tours of Belleville, Ménilmontant, Canal Saint-Martin, Oberkampf, Goutte-d'Or, Pantin or Saint-Ouen lasting two to two and a half hours.

BY BIKE

Paris à Vélo C'est Sympa (☎ 01 48 87 60 01; www.parisvelosympa.com; 22 Rue Alphonse Baudin, 11th; Ⓜ Saint-Sébastien Froissart) Offers tours of the capital by bike, avoiding the stressful traffic, in a variety of languages (English, Spanish, Italian…).

Paris Charms & Secrets (☎ 01 40 29 00 00; www.parischarmssecrets.com; meets at Place Vendôme, 1st; M Tuileries). Four-hour tours on electric bicycles.

THEMED TOURS

Guided tours that take visitors off the beaten track:

Not a Tourist Destination (☎ 01 40 27 82 11; www.notatouristdestination.com) A range of three-hour themed visits (culinary, shopping, kids…), in groups of eight people (€95/75 adult/child).

Design à Paris (☎ 01 74 30 16 75; www.designaparis.com). Three-hour walking tour of the Haut-Marais focusing on design (€75/person, min 4 people; ☻ Sat 2-6pm).

Taxi Tram (☎ 01 53 19 73 50; www.tram-idf.fr; taxitram@tram-idf.fr). Open-topped tour exploring contemporary art in the Île-de-France region held on one Saturday every month (€5/person).

HOLIDAYS

New Year's Day 1 January
Easter Sunday end March/April
Easter Monday end March/April
May Day 1 May
Victory in Europe Day 8 May
Ascension Thursday May
Whit Monday May/June
Bastille Day 14 July
Assumption Day 15 August
All Saints' Day 1 November
Armistice Day 11 November
Christmas Day 25 December

MONEY

CREDIT CARDS

Visa is the most widely accepted credit card, followed by

MasterCard. American Express and Diners Club are only accepted in the most exclusive establishments.

CHANGING MONEY

Visitors from outside the Eurozone can change currency in major train stations and hotels. Post offices also exchange currency at reasonable rates. In general, banks charge commission of €3 to €4.50 per transaction.

The following bureaux de change are open from 10am to 5.45pm:

Le Change du Louvre (☎ 01 42 97 27 28; www.changedulouvre.com; 151 Rue Saint-Honoré, 1st; M Palais Royal–Musée du Louvre; ☻ 10am-6pm Mon-Fri)

Banque Travelex (☎ 01 47 20 25 14; 125 Av des Champs-Élysées, 8th; M Charles de Gaulle–Étoile; ☻ 9am-8pm Mon-Sat, 10am-7pm Sun)

NEWSPAPERS

Daily papers like *Le Parisien* or the free *À Nous Paris*, *Lylo* and certain magazines, including *Télérama* and *Les Inrockuptibles*, provide useful information on Paris' cultural happenings.

PARIS MUSEUM PASS

If you plan on visiting a number of museums, it might be worth investing in a **Paris Museum Pass** (www.parismuseumpass.com), which is valid for 2/4/6 days (€32/48/64). It gives access to more than 60 museums, and allows you to bypass the queues. Passes are available from tourist offices, participating museums and monuments and Fnac shops.

SHOW TICKETS

Tickets for concerts, the theatre and sporting events are sold at **Fnac** (www.fnac.com) and the **Virgin Megastore** (www.virginmega.fr), on-line or in the stores. You can also try the agency **Cultival** (☎ 0825 05 44 05; www.cultival.fr).

If you haven't booked a ticket, you can check if there are any unsold seats offered at half-price (plus commission of around €2.50) on the day of the performance at the following outlets:

Kiosque Théâtre Madeleine (opposite 15 Place de la Madeleine, 8th; 🕑 12.30-7.45pm Tue-Sat, to 3.45pm Sun; Ⓜ Madeleine)

Montparnasse Kiosque Théâtre (Parvis Montparnasse, 14th; 🕑 12.30-7.45pm Tue-Sat, to 3.45pm Sun; Ⓜ Montparnasse-Bienvenüe).

Discounted tickets are available on-line at www.billetreduc.com and www.ticketac.com.

SMOKING

As of January 2008, smoking is banned in all public places, bars and restaurants.

TELEPHONE
DIALLING CODES

To call France from abroad, dial the international call code followed by the dialling code for France ☎ 33 and the 10-digit number of the person you want to call (omitting the initial 0). The dialling code for Paris and the surrounding area is ☎ 01.

To call overseas from France, dial ☎ 00 followed by the overseas country code.

USEFUL NUMBERS

International directory enquiries (☎ 32 12)
Local directory enquiries (☎ 118 710; 118 712) Full list of information services available at www.allo118.com.

MOBILE PHONES

France uses the GSM 900/1800 mobile phone system, which is incompatible with the GSM 1900 system used in North America (except for GSM 1900/900 mobiles).

Public telephones require phonecards (€7.50), which are available at post offices, *tabacs*, supermarkets, SNCF ticket windows, metro stations and anywhere you see the blue sticker *'télécarte en vente ici'*.

TIPPING

Hotels, cafés and restaurants are required by law to include service on their bills (usually 15%). Tipping is therefore not expected, although some people choose to leave a couple of euros.

DIRECTORY

TRAVELLERS WITH DISABILITIES

 Sites bearing this label guarantee reliable information, a specially adapted reception and facilities for disabled visitors. Close to 200 sites in Paris and the Île-de-France region have this label.

The Paris metro is not accessible to wheelchair users, with the exception of line 14. Access ramps are few and far between, but due to new legal requirements, can now be found in recently constructed museums, hotels, and public buildings.

Many restaurants only have partially adapted facilities, with toilets, in particular, often not properly fitted out – check when making reservations.

INFORMATION & ORGANISATIONS

Comprehensive information for travellers with reduced mobility can be found on the website of the **Paris Île-de-France Tourist Board** (www.new-paris -idf.com). For all information on the accessibility of public transport, refer to the *Guide Pratique à l'Usage des Personnes à Mobilité Réduite* (Practical Guide for People with Reduced Mobility), published by the **Syndicat des Transports d'Île-de-France** (☎ 01 47 53 28 00; www.stif-idf.info).

TRANSPORT
ARRIVAL & DEPARTURE
TRAIN

Paris has six mainline train stations, all of which are accessible by metro: Gare d'Austerlitz, Gare de l'Est, Gare de Lyon, Gare du Nord, Gare Montparnasse and Gare Saint-Lazare.

Information is available from the SNCF (Société Nationale des Chemins de Fer; ☎ 36 35; www.sncf.com) and tickets for all French trains and the main high-speed trains in Europe (such as TGV, Eurostar, Thalys) can be booked at www.tgv-europe.com.

Eurostar (☎ 35 35; www.eurostar.com) takes you from Paris–Gare du Nord to London–St Pancras International in two hours 15 minutes. **Thalys** (www .thalys.com) links Paris–Gare du Nord with Bruxelles-Midi, Amsterdam CS and Cologne-Hauptbahnhof.

AIR

Paris is a destination of almost all international airlines. The Aéroports de Paris site (www.adp.fr) provides information on flights, routes and carriers.

The two major international airports, **Roissy Charles de Gaulle** and **Orly** are linked to central Paris by various modes of transport; the most practical options are listed below. Further out, **Paris-Beauvais**, which is connected by a bus service, is used by charter companies and budget airlines such as Ryanair.

Roissy-Charles de Gaulle Airport

The larger of the two airports, **Roissy-Charles de Gaulle** (☎ 39 50; www.adp.fr) is 30km northest of central Paris. There is a free shuttle between the two terminals, CDG1 and CDG2, every six minutes.

RER

The two terminals are served by Roissy Rail on RER line B3. Trains to the city centre depart every 15 minutes from 5.30am to midnight (€8.20 single) and take 40 minutes (Saint-Michel, Châtelet and Gare du Nord stations).

Bus

Cars Air France (☎ 08 92 35 08 20; www.cars-airfrance.com; single/return €15/24) Makes several stops in Paris.
Noctilien (www.noctilien.fr; one ticket per zone crossed) Buses leave every hour from 12.30am to 5.30am: the N121 stops at Montparnasse, Châtelet, Gare du Nord; the N140 stops at Gare du Nord and Gare de l'Est.
Roissybus (€9.10 single) Links the airport and Rue Scribe, Place de l'Opéra. The journey lasts between 45 and 60 minutes and buses run from 5.45am to 11pm.

Airport shuttle

For door-to-door service by private shuttles, such as the **Paris Airports Service** (☎ 01 55 98 10 80; 1 person €25, 2 or more people €15/person).

Taxi

Expect to pay between €40 and €55 for a 50-minute journey depending on traffic.

Orly Airport

Orly (☎ 39 50; www.adp.fr), 18km south of central Paris, has two terminals, *Ouest* (mainly for internal flights) and *Sud*, linked by a free rail shuttle, Orlyval.

RER

The **Orlyval** train (☎ 32 46; www.orlyval.com; single ticket € 9.60) links Orly to RER line B at Antony in the space of eight minutes, every seven minutes from 6am to 11pm. From Antony, it takes 35 minutes to reach the city centre (Saint-Michel, Châtelet and Gare du Nord stations).

Bus

Noctilien (www.noctilien.fr; one ticket per zone crossed) The N31 runs every hour from 12.30am to 5.30am and connects Gare de Lyon, Place d'Italie and Gare d'Austerlitz to Orly-Sud.
Orlybus (€6.30 single) takes around 30 minutes to reach Place Denfert-Rochereau (14th). Buses leave every 15 to 20 minutes from 6am to 11.30pm from Paris; and from 5.35am to 11pm from the airport.

Airport shuttle

The bus **Air France 1** (☎ 0892 35 08 20; single/return €11.50/18.50) links the airport with Gare Montparnasse in 30 to 45 minutes, every 30 minutes from 6.15am to 11.15pm, and with Aérogare des Invalides and Place de l'Étoile from 6am to 11.30pm.

Taxi
A taxi costs between €40 and €45 (depending on travel time) and takes at least 30 minutes.

Paris-Beauvais Airport
Situated 80km to the north of Paris, **Paris-Beauvais** airport (☎ 0892 68 20 66; www.aeroportbeauvais.com) is used by charter companies and Ryanair.

Bus
An express service leaves the airport every 20 to 30 minutes each time a flight arrives, from 5.45am to 7.15pm, and drops off passengers at Place de la Porte Maillot. In the opposite direction, buses leave Paris three hours 15 minutes before flight departures from **Pershing car park** (1 blvd Pershing, 17th; Ⓜ Porte Maillot).

Tickets (☎ information 0892 682 064; single €14, 75 min) are on sale in the arrival lounge at the airport or directly at the kiosk in the bus car park.

Taxi
A taxi between central Paris and Beauvais costs around €110 during the day and €150 at night and on Sundays.

COACH
Eurolines (☎ 01 43 54 11 99, 0892 89 90 91; www.eurolines.com) offers coach services towards all of Europe: the **Gare Routière Internationale de Paris-Gallieni** (☎ 0892 89 90 91; 28 Av du Général de Gaulle; Ⓜ Gallieni) is just at the edge of Bagnolet.

GETTING AROUND
Walking is by far the best way to explore Paris, but the city has a reliable, efficient and speedy public transport network, managed by the **RATP** (Régie Autonome des Transports Parisiens; www.ratp.fr). Public transport stations closest to the sites listed are marked with the Ⓜ symbol.

TRAVEL PASSES
Mobilis and Paris Visite travel passes are valid on the metro, the RER, SNCF suburban lines, buses, night buses, trams and the Montmartre cable-car.

Paris Visite (www.ratp.info/touristes) allows you to make an unlimited number of journeys in zones 1 to 3 or 1 to 6, and grants access to certain museums, as well as other discounts and benefits. A three-zone travel pass costs €9/14.70/20/28.90 for 1/2/3/5 days. A six-zone travel pass (including service to the two airports) costs €18.90/28.90/40.50/49.40. Passes are sold at major metro and RER stations, SNCF shops and airports.

The **Carte Mobilis** (www.ratp.fr, see under 'tous les tarifs') grants unlimited travel one day for between two and six zones (from €5.90 for one to two zones). Available at metro, RER and SNCF stations in the Paris region.

METRO, RER, TRAIN & TRAM

The underground train network is the quickest way to get around Paris. It is made up of two interconnected networks: the metro with a total of 14 lines and 372 stations, and the RER (Réseau Express Régional) consisting of five lines (A to E) with services between the city centre and the suburbs.

Each metro line is identified by a number, a colour and a destination (also indicated on the platform). Most services start at around 5.30am and the last train leaves between 12.35am and 1am. The metro runs until 2.15am on Friday and Saturday and the night before public holidays. Metro and bus lines cover the smallest recesses of the city.

There are three **tram** lines (www .tramway.paris.fr), two serving the suburbs, and the new T3, which links the 13th, 14th and 15th arrondissements (Left Bank).

A ticket valid for use within Paris costs €1.60 (€1.70 in the bus) or €11.60 for a carnet of 10 tickets. The type and price of tickets for journeys outside Paris depend on the destination. A ticket allows you to make any journey within a two-hour period, regardless of the number of changes. You can use these tickets on the RER inside zone 1, on buses or trams (but you cannot change from one to the other).

Information about public transport within Paris and in the Île-de-France can be found on the **RATP site** (www.ratp.fr) and on **Transilien SNCF** (www.transilien.com), which provides all information on travelling in Île-de-France by the RER or train.

BOAT

The river shuttles **Batobus** (☎ 0825 05 01 01; www.batobus.com; 1 day € 13/7; Ⓜ Bir Hakeim) criss-cross the Seine between the Eiffel Tower and the Jardin des Plantes, making eight stops along the way. Departures from the Port de la Bourdonnais every 25 to 30 minutes from 10am. No service from beginning of Jan to beginning of Feb. The **Voguéo** shuttle (p21) completes the fleet at the east of the Seine.

BUS

Buses run fairly frequently between 5.45am and 8.30pm and, on a more limited number of routes, in the evening and on Sundays. A route map and timetables can be obtained from the RATP.

The **Noctilien** night buses (www .noctilien.fr) run after the metro closes (see the web site for information and route map). The 27 routes cover almost all neighbourhoods. Short journeys cost one metro ticket, longer trips require two tickets.

CYCLING AND VÉLIB'

In addition to the bike trails of the Bois de Boulogne and Bois de Vincennes, many of Paris' streets have cycle lanes.

Facilities (cycle paths, separate cycle lanes, bus lanes…) are increasingly being provided. The banks of the Seine are closed to motorists on Sundays and public holidays, from 9am to 5pm (every day from 15 July to 15 August), for the benefit of cyclists.

Vélib' (☎ 01 30 79 79 30; www.velib.paris .fr) is a self-service bike hire system, ideal for short journeys. Subscriptions are payable at service points by bank card (Visa, JCB, MasterCard and American Express). A short-term Vélib' subscription costs €1 for one day (24 hours from the time the bike is taken from the terminal) and € 5 for seven days. The first half-hour is free (return your Vélib' to a terminal before the first 30 minutes are up); after that it costs €1 for the next half-hour, €2 more for the next half-hour and €4 from the third half-hour.

A deposit of €150 is required, given by means of pre-authorisation to withdraw the funds from your bank account (not cashed). That said, when you return your Vélib', make sure it is properly attached to its terminal and collect the receipt proving that you have returned it (essential if you have to make a claim).

The **Vinci** network (www.vincipark.com) also offers a bike-hire service to customers from its car parks.

For cycling news in Paris, visit www .paris.fr, under *'vélos et circulation douce'* (bicycles and non-motorised transport). See p153 for guided bike tours of Paris.

TAXI

There is no shortage of taxis in Paris, but securing one can be difficult, particularly on Saturday evenings. Your best bet is to try one of the ranks that sit alongside most of the major intersections.

The initial fee is €2 and the rate within central Paris is €0.77/km between 7am and 7pm from Monday to Saturday (tariff A, white light on the meter), and €1.09/km from 7pm to 7am and all day on Sundays and public holidays (tariff B, orange light on the meter). In the suburbs, tariff C is €1.31/km.

A €2.60 supplement is charged for a fourth passenger, but most drivers refuse to take more than three passengers for insurance reasons. Luggage weighing more than 5kg adds €1, as does pick-up from a station.

If you want to reserve a taxi, all ranks that have phones can be contacted on ☎ 01 45 30 30 30. A voice server allows you to select your arrondissement and the closest rank.

CAR

Several hire companies have offices at Roissy Charles de Gaulle Airport and in the city:
Ada ☎ 01 42 03 64 40; www.ada.fr
Avis ☎ 08 20 05 05 05; www.avis.fr
Europcar ☎ 0825 825 457; www.europcar.fr
Hertz ☎ 01 55 31 93 21; www.hertz.fr

>INDEX

See also separate subindexes for See (p163), Shop (p164), Eat (p165), Drink (p166) and Play (p167).

000 map pages

🍴 EAT

000 map pages